fresh

strong

inspiring

Waterside Productions, Inc.
2376 Oxford Avenue
Cardiff-by-the-Sea, CA 92007
www.waterside.com

Editor: Celia Sepulveda, Ph. D.
Food Stylist: Constance Pikulas
Assistants: Dana Ecelberger, Amanda Guthrie, Jennifer Pruett
Book Design and Layout: Donald Kilgore and Adam Stacoviak – IMAGE202 ENTERTAINMENT, www.IMAGE202.com
Book Photography: Talitha Bullock and Donald Kilgore – IMAGE202 ENTERTAINMENT, and domenica catelli
Front Cover & Bio Photos: Tim Klein, www.timkleinphoto.com

Additional photos: Daphne Plug – DDP Photography (page 130), Tami DeSellier, www.tamiland.com (page 9), Josh Rose (pages 40, 92)

ISBN 978-1-933754-14-7

Library of Congress Cataloging-in-Publication Data

Catelli, Domenica
mom-a-licious

Control Number: 2007928227

Printed in Canada

10 9 8 7 6 5 4 3 2

domenica catelli

for my family

table of contents

foreword

Feeding our families great food can be delicious fun!

As a pediatrician, I've had contact with millions of parents regarding the health of their children. Over the years I've learned that one of the biggest headaches for many moms is trying to ensure good nutrition for their children. Whether it is because of the food battles (refusing to eat vegetables on principle) or products that are trendy and regaled as healthy (soda with vitamins?), the struggle can become exhausting. But this book is full of good news.

There's no reason to be limited to choosing between enduring endless food battles and settling for hydrogenated, over-processed, junk fare. Mom-a-licious celebrates another way – full of zest, laughter, and the joy of great food.

I used to think that when weaning was complete, "perfect food" was over for babies, and for all of us. Then it dawned on me – as surely as young babies are designed for milk, the rest of us (toddlers, soccer players, school kids and their busy parents) are designed to thrive eating a fantastic variety of fruits, vegetables, whole grains, and more. There are perfect foods for us, designed to be delicious and satisfying, while supplying a complex array of nutrients in a simple, creative, natural way. And the whole process provides a throng of side benefits for us and our families.

When you give children good nutrition, you are giving them the nutrient building blocks that literally become the eyes you look into; the bones that support their growing bodies; their inquisitive, curious brains; and the hearts that pump quietly night and day through the years.

The instinct to nurture and protect our families is saucy and sure. It moves to rhythms more ancient than memory, more hip than tomorrow. Listen for the beat.

In this beautiful book, domenica catelli leads the way in a dance of discovery, through grocery store aisles, around our kitchens, and into the heart of parenting.

She provides recipes that people can count on – they are good for you, they are quick and easy, and taste great. She has creative, healthy solutions for baby's first foods (avocado quinoa mash – yum!) as well as vegetables to serve with dinner that your kids will love. She knows what is on your plate, literally and figuratively, and helps take away the guilt, confusion, and exhaustion so many parents feel.

Join the thousands of parents who have learned from domenica – be mom-a-licious, and be proud of the way you feed your family.

Alan Greene, MD, FAAP
www.DrGreene.com

dr. greene

Dr. Alan Greene is one of the world's most trusted and beloved pediatricians. He is a graduate of Princeton University and the University of California at San Francisco, and a father of four. His award-winning site, DrGreene.com, receives over 50 million hits a month from parents, concerned family members, students, and healthcare professionals. He loves to think about challenging ideas, he collects encyclopedias, and he wears green socks.

introduction

You are mom-a-licious! You are strong, creative and loving. You care for your family, live your life, and try to stay on top of everything from education, to budgets and soccer practice. But there is part of being mom-a-licious that sometimes gets lost in the shuffle. When we slip into our oversized, stretched-out sweats before hitting the drive-through, then we are not living up to our potential. We all need to reignite that mom-a-licious spark that lives inside each of us. This book is about rediscovering what we may have buried under piles of laundry, sleep deprivation, and being nurturing to everyone but ourselves. I am going to give you some pointers on what to introduce to your pantry, accessible recipes, and quick tips that will empower and inspire you to live mom-a-liciously!

I have worked with many families who have changed their eating habits and have been rewarded with increased energy, smaller waistlines, fewer toddler meltdowns, and greater confidence and pride in their cooking. This book shares the principles of creating a nutritional environment that I've used to ensure a healthy more vital lifestyle for my family.

As a starting point, you will want to take a look at your pantry, refrigerator and freezer, and embrace some mom-a-licious essentials. With my recipes, you will learn new ways to start the morning that boost energy and sustain you through lunch. Soups, grain salads, and dips will broaden lunch horizons. Finally, the daunting question of "how do I get my kids to eat more vegetables?" will be answered using tasty ingredients and simple-to-prepare recipes for dinner.

Beyond the pantry makeovers, grocery store outings and great recipes, there are tips sprinkled throughout the book on how to recover and retain your spark, fire, and cool while keeping your family and yourself well-nourished, in body and soul. This book starts with the **mom-a-licious** manifesto, and exemplifies the core virtues of motherhood today.

domenica catelli

domenica catelli

mom-a-licious manifesto

mom-a-licious is more than just cooking... it is a lifestyle!

1. **Know** what is in your food and where it comes from – if an ingredient has more than four syllables, it probably doesn't belong in the human body.

2. Eat and serve local and **organic** as much as possible.

3. Grow something fresh and use it – whether you have a large **garden** or one potted herb.

4. **Resist** tantrum-folding (caving in) when your child fights you over a vegetable, bed time, or the sugary cereal they must have.

5. Style is personal expression, use it. Whether it's wearing signature pearls or vibrant green when the **fashion** magazines are trying to convince you that mauve is a must-have, make a statement that is uniquely "you." Show the world who you are!

6. Revive family **traditions** – they are your family's unique mark on the world; no one else has the same take on food, celebrations, crafts, song, dance, and gatherings.

7. Have **fun** with your kids. The best part of having kids is feeling young again: laughter, goofiness, playing hide & seek, and Saturday-morning kisses. Avoid over-programming. Sure, you are stressed, just don't let them feel it.

8. Go out with your **friends** regularly, let off steam, make memories, and come home grateful for your family.

9. Be an **advocate** for your family: make healthy food choices, set aside dedicated time together, spend time in nature, and turn off the TV and really connect.

10. **Learn** something new about something that scares you. Is it kale that scares you? Or public speaking? Read voraciously, and ask questions.

11. Make **quality time** for your beloved. You have picked each other for a reason, so take time to nurture and rejuvenate your connection.

12. Tell someone they **inspire** you, whether it is your mom, your child, your cousin, or someone you have been too intimidated to approach – we need to support one another.

13. Get out of any ruts and **get moving**. Not exercising enough, watching too much TV, or going through the drive-through for dinner? Make the needed changes and live your best life, today.

14. **Ask for help**. Whether it is folding laundry, doing errands, or picking up the kids from school – you are not alone and your friends want to help. Giving is good for us, and letting others give to us is sometimes the best gift we could offer them.

15. Make time to build health and **strength** – we want to be around to enjoy our kids and set the example that health is essential. Plus, it is fun and energizing to get your body moving!

16. Live with **gratitude**. Whether it is taking time when you wake up, before you eat or at the end of the day, take note of your blessings and give thanks!

pantry 101

One of the essentials to living a mom-a-licious life is to be aware of what is in your pantry, refrigerator, and freezer. After all, you carefully consider the influence of all kinds of things in your family's life: friends, television, and the Internet. It is time to do some inventory on the chemicals, salts, preservatives, and dyes that lurk within feet of your loved ones.

If you start to feel that you need a degree in higher chemistry to decipher the ingredients in the foods currently residing in your kitchen, chances are I'm going to tell you to take it out. There is an organic or fresh alternative to almost all of your usual snacks.

DON'T BE SCARED! I know that this process can be intimidating and you might think that you will end up with a naked pantry after this exercise. If you are feeling like it is too much to take on, then hold on! I would rather you change one thing a week than do nothing. I've had some friends that started by taking out hydrogenated oil products. I then started challenging them about corn syrup and artificial sweeteners (what are good friends for?). They are now proud of having well-stocked, mom-a-licious pantries. I promise that you too will feel a newfound freedom. The reality is that you and I know when we are making bad choices for ourselves and our families. We do it for a variety of reasons, but we pay a price, and we lose a bit of that mom-a-licious spark when we make choices that don't support our family's health and wellness. Get ready and cut yourself loose from any intimidation that might be plaguing you and repeat after me, "I am not a bad mom."

Are you ready?

a fresh start

reclaiming the pantry

kick out:

- artificial sweeteners (even if they are made from "real sugars")
- corn syrup
- refined sugars
- hydrogenated or partially hydrogenated oil
- dyes (especially red #3 and #40, and yellow #5)
- enriched flours (the flour is stripped of all nutrients and then added back in artificially)
- bleached flours
- canned vegetables (except tomatoes and beans)
- sugary cereals (candy for breakfast)
- fake fruit snacks for kids (these are usually loaded with corn syrup, dye, and hydrogenated oil)
- potatoes in a box
- instant rice
- peanut butters filled with sugar, corn syrup, and hydrogenated oil
- powdered and/or processed chocolate drinks

Now, doesn't that feel better? Or have you begun to panic because you have been enjoying some of those unhealthy foods for years? Just relax and breathe. Enjoy the fact that natural, unprocessed foods are your best defense against obesity, cancer, and ADD. It may be surprising how many seemingly harmless food choices can have so many preservatives. No need to dwell on the past — it is time to go shopping!

bring in:

- extra virgin olive oil (I use Lucini)
- pure maple syrup
- lentils
- beans
- whole grains (quinoa, bulgur, steel-cut oats, brown rice)
- natural peanut and almond butters
- dry spices: granulated garlic, cinnamon, cumin, curry powder, dried dill, peppercorns
- kosher salt
- good-quality dark chocolate
- dried mushrooms
- organic chicken broth
- a few pasta varieties (whole wheat Penne Rigate and egg noodles are good choices)
- good quality canned tuna or salmon, packed in water
- balsamic vinegar
- Pinot Grigio or champagne vinegar
- rice wine vinegar
- tamari

facing the refrigerator

Now that you have cleared the pantry and filled it with healthy, preservative-free foods, it is time to do the same in your refrigerator and freezer.

kick out:

- ☐ low-fat mayo (check the ingredients...less fat, but more sugar and chemicals. If you are going to use regular mayo, just use less)
- ☐ fake butter spreads (loaded with synthetic ingredients...again, it is better to use a SMALL amount of butter)
- ☐ soda, diet and regular
- ☐ processed lunch meats
- ☐ American cheese
- ☐ salad dressings with hydrogenated oil
- ☐ canned Parmesan cheese
- ☐ candy bars
- ☐ sugary "fruit" juices/drinks

The mere exercise of clearing your shelves will help you breathe deeper and easier. It is time to bring in the healthy fresh foods that will add new vitality to your family, and increase the confidence that comes with building a healthier home.

bring in:

- ☐ organic milk (if you are going to do only one thing organic, start here!)
- ☐ organic kefir (I use Lifeway and Helios brands)
- ☐ organic butter
- ☐ organic plain yogurt
- ☐ organic, free-range eggs
- ☐ cheese (real Parmesan, raw cheddar, Brie)
- ☐ hummus
- ☐ herb and/or sun-dried tomato pesto
- ☐ apples
- ☐ citrus (lemons and limes, grapefruits, tangerines)
- ☐ melons, in season
- ☐ broccoli
- ☐ carrots
- ☐ sweet potatoes
- ☐ celery
- ☐ arugula
- ☐ grape tomatoes
- ☐ garlic
- ☐ onions
- ☐ fresh herbs (parsley, cilantro, basil, rosemary, mint and dill)
- ☐ nitrate-free turkey
- ☐ Bragg's liquid aminos
- ☐ grain mustard
- ☐ miso
- ☐ tofu
- ☐ unsweetened juice (mix with sparkling water for a soda substitute)
- ☐ sparkling water

facing the freezer

There really are only a few evils lurking in the freezer, but they are important to face and discard.

kick out:

- [ ] frozen prepared meals with high sodium and synthetic ingredients
- [ ] frozen treats with hydrogenated oil, dyes, and corn syrup

bring in:

- [ ] frozen organic berries (strawberries, blueberries, raspberries)
- [ ] frozen bananas
- [ ] frozen sweet organic corn
- [ ] frozen organic peas
- [ ] edamame beans
- [ ] a few one-pound packs of chicken breast tenders
- [ ] wrapped sandwiches made for lunch (see page 51)
- [ ] homemade soups, sauces, and pestos
- [ ] whole grain bread and English muffins (I like Ezekiel 4:9 and California Bakery). Breads without preservatives can mold quickly when left in the pantry or on the counter. The refrigerator will dry them out, so store in the freezer.

For updated lists and further recommendations, go to www.mom-a-licious.com

grocery 101

demystifying the grocery store

Milk, eggs, bread, chicken. This is what screams out to us when we are on autopilot in the grocery store.

There are so many exciting choices at your fingertips, yet just as many dangerous ones. By embracing the pantry and refrigerator basics on the previous pages, you are on your way to a mom-a-licious kind of market experience!

Look at these five simple steps to getting the most out of your shopping.

- Eat seasonally as much as possible. If it is snowing outside you probably aren't going to find the best fresh tomatoes or blueberries around. You can talk to your grocer, or go to mom-a-licious.com to get your seasonal list.

- Break out of the mold. Try something new every week... whether it is quinoa, mango or a turnip, you will be expanding your family's taste buds. If you haven't tried a radish since you were four because your Great Aunt Mable used to serve them and you thought they were "icky,"get over it and try again!

- Look for grains, nuts and spices in bulk...you will be saving money and can keep your supply of foods fresher.

- Try fresh fish...there is a world of delicious seafood outside of frozen, breaded sticks! Try a market with a knowledgeable fishmonger and ask what is freshest and mildest in flavor.

- Get your kids involved in choosing foods outside of the cereal or snack aisle...Have them pick the new vegetables or fruits you are going to try this week. Engaging children in these choices will make introducing new foods easier.

defined, decoded & demystified

beans

dry vs. canned

I am not a fan of many things from a can but beans are one of the exceptions. You do not get the depth of flavor as you would when cooking with dry beans, but you do save hours of time. Beans are high in protein and inexpensive.

brine

Traditionally a strong solution of salt and water used to pickle or preserve foods. When brining for a shorter period it can serve to cut down cooking times on meats such as pork, turkey, and chicken as well as adding flavor and helping to retain moisture. Sugar, molasses, citrus, and spices can be added as well.

brewer's yeast (or nutritional yeast)

Yellow, flakey, and nutty in flavor. Found mainly in natural food stores, it is very high in B vitamins. Great with potatoes, on toast, in soups, or with veggies.

cous cous

Cous cous is a simple and quick cooking side dish. It is actually pasta, usually made from semolina flour. You can also try it in whole wheat or Israeli style (much larger size).

extra virgin olive oil (not all virgins are created equal)

If you are at the supermarket and you see extra virgin olive oil for $5 a gallon, then steer clear! You are not getting what you think. Usually when an oil is that low in price it is most likely very low-quality. The health benefits of a high-quality oil are phenomenal, and it adds and enhances flavor. Cheap oil taints flavor and does not have the integrity that you deserve in your food.

flaxseed

One of the richest sources of omega-3, but is also high in calcium, iron, and vitamin E. It is great to add to smoothies, cereals, or salads. You need to use it in a ground form to obtain the nutrtional benefits.

freeze your bananas

One of the greatest additions to smoothies. The frozen banana adds a creamy texture while providing a mega boost of potassium. I slice up and throw the overripe bananas (I never get around to making banana bread with these) into a sealable plastic bag in the freezer for easy access.

freeze your sandwiches

The best time saver for packing lunches. You can't freeze lettuce or tomato but you can freeze turkey, pb & j, ab & j, and cheese sandwiches.

frozen vs. fresh

Fresh should always be the choice for produce when in season. However, if you want blueberries in December in Iowa, I would only recommend them in frozen organic form. Frozen fruit is picked when it is ripe, so the flavor and nutrients have had time to develop. Unfortunately, some fresh fruits and veggies are picked when they haven't ripened, and are sent to ripen in the store. This sacrifices flavor and nutrition.

granulated garlic

Dried and then ground garlic. This is a must-have staple in the pantry. It provides a quick boost of flavor to veggies, sauces, egg dishes, dressings, and garlic bread. It is not the same as garlic salt or powdered garlic.

heavy-bottomed pans

These distribute heat evenly, which means that your soup, sauce, or snapper won't be burnt on the bottom and under-cooked on the top.

honey

Local, raw honey can help with allergies. This natural sweetener is great in everything from yogurt to marinades.

kosher salt

Kosher salt is large-grained and additive-free. You also use less salt when using kosher because the grains stay on top of the food making it easy to taste. Also, unlike table salt, kosher salt has no additives to make it free flowing.

defined, decoded & demystified (continued)

kefir

This is one of my favorite refrigerator staples. The consistency is between milk and yogurt. Kefir is packed with protein, calcium and probiotics (probiotics help with everything from inhibiting food allergies for children, to building a strong immune system, and preventing yeast infections). Although kefir is a dairy product, it is safe for those who are lactose intolerant. I use kefir in smoothies, salad dressings, baking, and in fish, chicken and meat dishes.

kosher salt

Kosher salt is large-grained and additive-free. You also use less salt when using kosher because the grains stay on top of the food making it easy to taste. Also, unlike table salt, kosher salt has no additives to make it free flowing.

maple syrup

Pure maple syrup enhances pancakes, baked goods, and smoothies. A little bit goes a long way and the flavor is phenomenal.

meyer lemons

Yum! Lower in acid and sweeter than regular lemons, these are available from December - May in specialty and farmers' markets. Use them in place of regular lemons. Also makes delicious lemonade.

microplane grater

A thin, hand-held grater. The best! Makes grating Parmesan, zesting lemons, or grating fresh nutmeg or ginger a cinch.

minced vs. chopped

Minced = cut into small pieces, and chopped = coarsely cut into small pieces, larger than a mince. You tend to mince garlic and chop an onion.

nutrient dense

Foods that have a high proportion of vitamins and minerals but have a lower number of calories.

portion size

I think we should admit it, fast food isn't the only place we are guilty of supersizing. Our portion sizes are starting to resemble small troughs. Keep the size down and slow down. Many times we are eating so fast that our brain hasn't received the message from our stomachs that we are full. Being mindful of quantity will keep waistlines down. It's usually the chips, cookies, and fries that you have to watch out for....you don't hear too much of, "You really need to cut down on the amount of green leafy vegetables you are eating."

quinoa (keen-wah)

One of my favorite underutilized foods. An ancient grain considered a super protein because it has all eight amino acids present; it also has the highest protein content of any grain. Quinoa cooks in half the time of rice and has a texture similar to cous cous. The general rule for cooking is a one-to-one ratio of liquid to quinoa. Make sure you rinse before cooking — this helps reduce any bitter taste.

raw nuts

It is true that nuts are high in fat, but they offer the kind of fat that our bodies need. Nuts lose many of their vital nutrients when they are toasted. If you aren't a fan of raw nuts, try mixing half roasted with half raw.

zest

The thin outer layer of citrus. Use only the colored part and avoid the white underpart (the pith).

breakfast the mom-a-licious way

I would be thrilled if drinking coffee was the most nutritious way to start the day. Unfortunately for me, and all the caffeine addicts out there, it's not.

Since I am 100% not a morning person, you can be assured that all of these morning recipes are painless to make. Most of them can be whipped up while you are mentally still half asleep. Yet, they are nutrient-dense, whole foods that will keep you energized and sustained throughout the morning.

By sending your kids off to school with a super cereal versus a "bowl of candy" (my affectionate name for most of the popular cereals) you are setting them up for better concentration and energy (sans the sugar crash) for their early classes.

If you have toddlers and wee ones, getting them going with the right balance in the morning will lead to fewer meltdowns for them (and for you).

blueberry and flaxseed smoothie

A smoothie is a great way to get a healthy serving of fruit on the go. By adding ground flaxseed you are adding great omega-3's that help with brain development and fighting cholesterol, without changing the flavor. Blueberries are packed with antioxidants. I use organic frozen berries because they are picked at their prime and have more flavor and vitamins than out-of-season berries. Surprisingly, they can also be less expensive. To give your smoothie a rich and creamy texture, use frozen bananas.

Ingredients

1 cup	fresh or organic frozen blueberries (or peaches, raspberries, & strawberries)
1	frozen banana
1 ½ cups	pomegranate or other unsweetened fruit juice
½ cup	plain organic kefir (or substitute plain yogurt)
1 tablespoon	ground flaxseed

optional: If you prefer it sweeter, add honey, maple syrup or agave nectar

the process

1. Put everything in the blender...enjoy.

quick tips

- Pour into popsicle molds for a frozen tasty treat

- Add a bit of soap and hot water to blender and run for twenty seconds, rinse. Clean up is done in under a minute!

- Remember to peel and cut up your over-ripe bananas and freeze them in sealable sandwich bags. Frozen bananas add texture and potassium in an instant and save you from the guilt of not getting around to making banana bread.

skylar's stinky-cheese breakfast sandwich

My goddaughter Skylar was introduced to little bits of artisanal cheeses at a very early age (10 months). At two-years old, Skylar enjoys a variety of tastes, textures and foods. The smallest amount of these great cheeses helps stimulate and broaden the palate - a true inoculation to fussy eating later! This recipe adds depth of flavor and complexity to basic eggs. Play around with different cheeses.

Ingredients (Serves 4)

2	whole eggs
4	egg whites
4	whole grain English muffins or eight slices whole grain bread (without corn syrup)
pinch	salt and fresh pepper
1 teaspoon	fresh thyme, finely chopped
slice	stinky cheese (Brie, Camembert, and Taleggio are great)

optional additions: tomato slices, basil leaves, turkey bacon, avocado, sweet and spicy mustard

the process

1. Put bread or English muffins in toaster while eggs are cooking.

2. Whisk eggs, salt and pepper and thyme together.

3. Heat a bit of extra virgin olive oil in a sauté pan and add eggs. Quickly scramble and be careful not to overcook.

4. Remove toasted bread and smear your choice of cheese on one side of the bread (less than a tablespoon per person).

5. Add your eggs and any other of your favorite options. I like to put sweet and spicy mustard on the other side of the bread. Wrap in wax paper and take on the road if you are in a rush.

quick steel-cut oats

Steel-cut oats are less processed than quick and rolled oats, leaving them higher in fiber. They are also much different in texture than common oats. By soaking your oats the night before, you cut the cooking time to $\frac{1}{3}$ of the normal time (traditionally, steel-cut oats take about 40 minutes to cook). Soaking breaks down the coating on the oats allowing you to absorb more of the nutrients. Steel-cut oats are filling and high in nutrition – they will give you and the kids sustained energy throughout the morning. We love to add fresh or frozen berries. You can make extra, refrigerate, and enjoy on other mornings.

Ingredients

1 cup	steel-cut oats
3 cups	water
pinch	salt
1 teaspoon	cinnamon

optional: milk, honey, nuts, fruit

the process

1. Before going to bed, fill a pot with one cup of water and oats and leave until morning.

2. When you are ready for breakfast, add two cups of water (or a mix of water and milk), cinnamon and a pinch of salt to the oats and let cook for 10-15 minutes.

3. Enjoy with warm milk, nuts (we like pecans and walnuts), blueberries, and maple syrup.

tofu and mushroom scramble

The curry powder gives a great color and depth of flavor to this easy breakfast alternative. If mushrooms and curry are an issue for the kids, you can omit. Add some cheese and a corn tortilla and you have a great breakfast taco.

Ingredients

½ cup	tofu, crumbled
1 teaspoon	garlic, granulated
1 teaspoon	curry powder (all curry powders are not created equal, if you have a strong one consider using ½ teaspoon and just a pinch for the small kids to get them acquainted with the flavor)
drizzle	extra virgin olive oil
½ cup	Crimini or button mushrooms, sliced
½ tablespoon	tamari, soy sauce or Bragg's liquid aminos

the process

1. Mix spices with tofu.

2. Heat a skillet and give a drizzle of extra virgin olive oil.

3. Add mushrooms and soy (or Bragg's) to pan.

4. When moisture starts to cook out of mushrooms add tofu and spices.

5. Cook, stirring constantly, until heated through (about 2 minutes).

Serve and enjoy!

super cereal

This cereal is super because it is packed with so many nutrients including fiber, protein, and amino acids. The addition of quinoa to breakfast provides all eight essential amino acids as well as a good amount of protein. Flaxseed provides omega-3's. Make extra and reheat during the week.

My friend Steven puts this on the stove in the morning and then showers, shaves and gets his daughters' lunches packed while this super cereal is cooking. When he is finished, he has a delicious and healthy breakfast ready for the family.

Ingredients

1 ½ cups	organic rolled oats *
½ cup	organic quinoa, rinsed
4 cups	water (or you can do ½ water and ½ milk or soy milk)
pinch	salt
½ teaspoon	cinnamon
1 tablespoon	ground flaxseed

optional: add dried fruit and drizzle of honey

the process

1. Place all ingredients (except flaxseed, dried fruit and honey) in a pan and bring to a boil.

2. Continue to simmer for 12-15 minutes.

3. Remove from heat and stir in flaxseed.

4. Serve with dried fruit and honey.

* If using quick oats start with the quinoa and liquid. Add the oats after the quinoa has cooked for 10 minutes and cook for five more minutes.

cardamom-citrus super cereal

This version of the super cereal adds cardamom, which lends an exotic flavor as well as providing magnesium and iron. The citrus adds a tangy dimension and extra vitamin C.

Ingredients

1 ½ cups	organic rolled oats
½ cup	organic quinoa, rinsed
1 cup	orange juice
3 cups	water
1	orange, zested
pinch	cardamom
1 tablespoon	ground flaxseed

optional: add dried fruit and drizzle of honey

the process

1. Place all ingredients (except flaxseed, dried fruit and honey) in a pan and bring to a boil.

2. Continue to simmer for 12-15 minutes.

3. Remove from heat and stir in flaxseed.

4. Serve with dried fruit and honey.

basic scramble 3 ways

Since I am NOT a morning person I like simple recipes that I don't have to think through and that don't have many steps. With that said, if you feel like eggs are too much to tackle in the a.m., let me assure you, these egg recipes are quick, painless and will provide you with valuable protein. My "secret" ingredient is a pinch of granulated garlic (this is the garlic you find in the spice aisle, make sure it is not powdered garlic or garlic salt). It adds a significant boost of flavor as well as vitamins A, B and C, and minerals like iron and calcium.

the basic eggs
Ingredients (per person)

drizzle	extra virgin olive oil
2 eggs	cracked into a small bowl (or one whole egg and two whites)
pinch	kosher salt
twist	fresh cracked pepper
pinch	granulated garlic

the process

1. Heat a skillet with a generous drizzle of extra virgin olive oil.

2. Whisk together eggs, salt, pepper and garlic.

3. Add to pan and continuously stir until cooked no more than two minutes – they will become overly dry if you cook too long.

mushroom
Ingredients

handful	Crimini or button mushrooms, sliced thin
pinch	granulated garlic hot pepper flakes

the process

1. Add the mushrooms to heated pan with the extra garlic and optional chili pepper flakes, add salt and pepper.

2. When the moisture has started to cook out of the mushrooms add your eggs and follow directions for basic eggs. You can also add one teaspoon of mixed-herb pesto (page 123).

sun-dried tomato pesto
Ingredients

½ tablespoon	sun-dried tomato pesto (see page 123)

the process

1. Add sun-dried tomato pesto to step one of basic egg recipe.

delicious & guiltless french toast

The traditional white bread French toast is packed with sugar, milk, refined carbohydrates and loaded with butter – a guilty pleasure, to be sure. This recipe is still delicious, but calls for whole grain bread (giving you complex carbohydrates) and egg whites to help keep cholesterol low. You can still use butter, but just a small amount – this way, you can enjoy the flavor without feeling bogged down afterwards. The kids love this healthy alternative and you will still feel like you are eating something decadent.

Ingredients (Serves 4, At One Slice Each)

8	egg whites	4 slices	whole grain bread (with no corn syrup or hydrogenated oil)
1 tablespoon	vanilla	slice	butter
¼ cup	orange juice (or juice from two oranges)		maple syrup and fresh berries
1 teaspoon	cinnamon		

the process

1. Mix eggs, orange juice, vanilla, and cinnamon together in a shallow dish.

2. Soak the piece of bread until it has absorbed most of the liquid. Heat a pan or griddle and add butter.

3. Put bread in pan, and pour remaining egg batter onto bread. Cook a few minutes, then flip.

4. Toast is done when both sides are golden. Top with fresh berries and pure maple syrup.

get the kids involved...

The weekend is a great time to get the **kids involved** in the kitchen. Take **10 minutes away from the morning cartoons** and have them join you in the kitchen to **crack some eggs** into the pancakes, **zest the orange** into the granola, or **whisk batter** for muffins. Start your weekend mornings with some **quality family time** while simultaneously creating memorable breakfast traditions.

citrus and sesame granola

I created this recipe when I was the Executive Chef at Raven's, located at the Stanford Inn in Mendocino, California. Add your favorite nuts and dried fruits, and if you don't like something in this ingredient list, omit it...you can use as many or as little nut varieties as you like - have fun making it your own! Make a batch on the weekend and you can enjoy throughout the week. Keep the granola in sealable plastic bags and put them in the car or wherever else you may be tempted to grab a treat. Raw nuts have more nutritional value than roasted ones, which is why you save part of them to add in at the end of the recipe.

Ingredients

2	lemons, zested	1 cup	raw cashews
½	lemon, juiced	½ cup	raw almonds
1½	orange, zested and juiced	½ cup	raw sunflower seeds
⅓ cup	extra virgin olive oil	¼ cup	raw sesame seeds
½ cup	pure maple syrup	½ cup	unsweetened dried coconut
	(or ¼ cup maple and ¼ cup honey)	¼ cup	flaxseed, ground
2	egg whites	1 cup	dried fruit
1 tablespoon	vanilla extract	½ cup	plain or flavored organic kefir
4 cups	organic rolled oats		

the process

Heat oven to 350 degrees.

1. Stir zest, juice, extra virgin olive oil, maple syrup, egg whites and vanilla together in a medium-sized bowl.
2. In a large bowl mix the oats, ½ of the nuts, ½ the sunflower seeds, all the sesame seeds and the coconut. Stir in syrup mixture.
3. Spread thinly on two cookie sheets covered in parchment paper or tinfoil for easy cleanup. Bake for 15 minutes then stir granola on trays with a wooden spoon. Continue to bake for seven more minutes or until golden brown.
4. Remove and cool. Stir in remaining nuts, flaxseed, and dried fruit.
5. When completely cooled, store in airtight containers and enjoy for up to a month, or keep in freezer for up to six months.
6. Serve with organic kefir and enjoy!

7

Have fun with your kids.

The best part of having kids is feeling young again:
laughter, goofiness, playing hide & seek, and
Saturday-morning kisses. Avoid over-programming.
Sure, you are stressed, just don't let them feel it.

hippie benedict

Eggs Benedict is one of my favorite things to eat when I'm out for breakfast. The large amount of butter that is in the sauce, the Canadian bacon and white bread make it a rare indulgence. This dish makes me feel like I'm having something extravagant without having to suffer through a butter hangover.

Ingredients (Per Serving)

1	egg
1	slice whole grain toast or ½ whole grain English muffin
	(Ezekiel 4:9 brand English muffins are my favorite for this)
1 cup	baby spinach
drizzle	extra virgin olive oil
pinch	salt & pepper

optional: sliced tomato and avocado

the process

1. Drizzle a small amount of olive oil in pan. Add spinach and salt. Sauté until wilted.

2. Bring a pan of water to a simmer. Stir water into a whirlpool.

3. Crack egg into whirlpool, cook for three to five minutes. Remove egg with a slotted spoon. Poach the egg so that the yolk is still runny and creates a "sauce" over the egg.

4. Toast the bread while egg is cooking. Layer with spinach.

5. Serve warm egg on top, and finish with salt and pepper.

* During the summer when tomatoes are ripe, substitute for spinach and add avocado.

pumpkin muffins

These muffins are delicious, easy to make, and great for you. Enjoy them hot out of the oven as well as keeping extra for lunchtime snacks for the kids (or you) during the week. Pumpkin is loaded with an important antioxidant, beta-carotene. Beta-carotene is one of the plant carotenoids converted to vitamin A in the body. In the conversion to vitamin A, beta-carotene performs many important functions in overall health. Current studies link diets rich in foods with beta-carotene to reducing the risk of certain types of cancer and protecting against heart disease.

Ingredients (Makes 12 Muffins)

1 cup	whole wheat or whole grain flour
½ cup	white unbleached flour
2 teaspoons	cinnamon
½ teaspoon	nutmeg
2 teaspoons	baking soda
½ teaspoon	salt
2	eggs
1 ½ cups	canned organic pumpkin (make sure there is only pumpkin in the ingredient list)
¼ cup	extra virgin olive oil
1 ¼ cups	maple syrup (or ½ cup agave nectar)
1 tablespoon	vanilla
½ cup	walnuts or pecans, chopped

the process

Pre-heat oven to 350 degrees.

1. Mix dry ingredients together in a bowl.

2. In a separate bowl mix all wet ingredients.

3. Fold the wet ingredients, (and fold in nuts if using) into the dry ingredients and spoon into paper-lined muffin or greased muffin tins.

4. Bake for 20 minutes or when toothpick inserted comes out clean. Remove to cool.

5. Store completely cooled muffins in sealable plastic bags in the freezer and pack in the kid's lunch.

ricotta and blackberry pancakes

The addition of ricotta cheese adds a fluffiness to the pancakes as well as extra protein. These pancakes are satisfying and filling. Frozen organic berries have a sweet flavor and can bring a burst of summer into the winter blues.

Ingredients (Makes 24-30 Small-Medium Sized Pancakes)

1 ⅓ cups	whole wheat flour
2 ½ teaspoons	baking powder
¼ teaspoon	salt
1 ½ cups	milk (whole or low fat)
1 cup	ricotta cheese (whole or low fat)
3 tablespoons	maple syrup plus more for topping
2	eggs
1 tablespoon	vanilla
1 cup	frozen or fresh blueberries or blackberries
bit	butter

the process

1. Whisk dry ingredients together (I use my four-cup measuring glass for this) .

2. In a separate bowl (or another four-cup measuring glass) whisk all wet ingredients together with the berries (including the three tablespoons of maple syrup).

3. Stir wet ingredients into dry ingredients. Add a bit more milk if batter is too thick. Heat a skillet or griddle over medium heat.

4. Add a teaspoon of butter and spread over the hot griddle.

5. Drop batter on a griddle one large tablespoon at a time. Flip when edges start to bubble.

6. Serve with warm maple syrup.

You can keep the pancakes warm in a 200 degree oven.

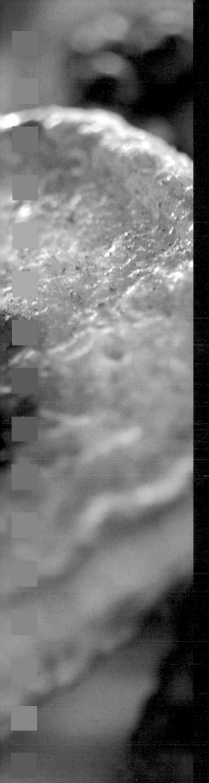

power pancakes (or waffles*) with blueberry "syrup"

By using multigrain flour with your pancakes you can check off a healthy serving of grains in your day. I love lemon in mine, but my husband is not a fan. If you have an anti-citrus member in your family separate out part of the batter and add the juice and zest to part of the batch. You can use this recipe in your waffle maker as well. If you like thinner, crepe-like pancakes then thin down the batter with a bit more juice.

Ingredients

pancakes

1 cup	multigrain flour
1 teaspoon	baking powder
pinch	salt
¾ cup	unsweetened apple juice
2	eggs
1	lemon, zested
2	lemons, juiced
bit	butter / extra virgin olive oil
	maple syrup

blueberry syrup

2 cups	frozen organic blueberries
2 tablespoons	water
3 tablespoons	honey
1	lemon, zested and juiced (if you use the lemon, omit the water)

the process (pancakes)

1. Stir dry ingredients together.

2. In a seperate bowl, whisk lemon and apple juice, zest and eggs together.

3. Fold in wet ingredients. Add a splash more juice if too dry.

4. Heat a skillet and add a small bit (about a ¼ inch slice) of butter or extra virgin olive oil then drop batter on one heaping tablespoon at a time.

5. Flip when edges brown. Serve with blueberry and maple syrup.

the process (syrup)

1. Put berries, honey and water (or juice and zest) in a small pot and turn on heat.

2. Cook until berries are soft, about five minutes.

3. Remove and purèe in a blender. Serve with pancakes and store extra in refrigerator for up to a week.

* If making waffles, add batter to waffle maker and cook according to manufacturer's instructions.

tasty and healthy lunch solutions

You know the frantic drill of making lunch **before your kids go off to school** with whatever leftovers you can find in the refrigerator, a juice box, and a salty bag of cheddar crackers – knowing full well they are not going to eat the leftovers.

Wouldn't it be comforting to know that your kids would eat a healthy serving of **protein or vegetables** each day without your supervision? These lunch recipes are designed to do just that.

lunch tips for eating on the go...

- Yes, you can pack a delicious salad. Try grilled chicken – make extra at dinner the night before and serve the next day to save time. Use chopped romaine, it stays crunchy and blends well with other ingredients including avocado, cherry tomato, and olives.

- Nobody likes squished or browned fruit. If you are going to cut fruit, use apples or pears and preserve with a squeeze of lemon or lime.

- Don't forget the hummus, vegetables, and crackers – can purchase or see recipe on page 58 for a quick and cost effective way to make your own.

- Have fresh fruits or vegetables at lunch to make you feel more energetic throughout the afternoon.

- For sandwiches, get the deli sliced meat vs. the processed. It is healthier (less preservatives) and has better flavor.

- Choose a non-hydrogenated snack (hydrogenated oils are linked to many health problems including heart disease and cancer).

- Freeze your sandwiches. We save time during the week making sandwiches on Sunday for the next week and freezing them. This works with turkey and cheese, pb & j, or ab & j (see page 54). You can't freeze lettuce or tomato, so keep these separate. Store the sandwiches in a sealable plastic bag. They will be thawed out by lunch and not the least bit soggy.

3-bean salad

Beans are one of the few foods out of a can that I will use. It saves hours of cooking time and the beans retain their nutrients. This recipe is crunchy, fresh, and full of protein and fiber.

Ingredients

1 can	kidney beans	1 teaspoon	celery seed (optional)
1 can	black beans	drizzle	extra virgin olive oil
1 can	chickpeas (garbanzo) beans	pinch	salt and pepper
2 ribs	celery, finely minced		
½ small	red onion, minced		
handful	flat leaf parsley, minced		
juice	of 2 lemons or		
2-3 tablespoons	vinegar		

optional: for a Latin flare, add lime, cilantro, large pinch of ground cumin, and minced jalapeño. You can also add chopped chicken.

the process

1. Drain and rinse beans and place in a large bowl.

2. Fold in celery, parsley and onion. Remember, you can add this at the very end if you want to omit for kids.

3. Stir in juice or vinegar, celery seed, salt and pepper and drizzle with extra virgin olive oil.

4. Taste and adjust for lemon and salt and pepper.

ab & j sandwich

I started my daughter at a young age with raw almond butter in her sandwiches instead of peanut butter. Almonds, especially raw, are very nutrient-dense. They are higher in manganese (an important antioxidant) and vitamin E than peanuts. Also, most peanut butters have added sugar and hydrogenated oil, which have no health benefit.

Ingredients (Per Serving)

2 slices	bread
2 tablespoons	almond butter
2 tablespoons	unsweetened jam or a drizzle of honey
1	banana, sliced

the process

1. Spread almond butter and jam on bread or layer with banana.

turkey and brie sandwich

You can make this sandwich with leftover chicken as well. Add some cranberry sauce and arugula to have that day-after Thanksgiving feeling anytime of the year. Arugula is a great leafy green and a wonderful source of nutrients, including iron.

Ingredients (Per Serving)

2 slices	whole grain bread or crusty French or sourdough roll
1 slice	Brie cheese
2 slices	turkey
several	arugula leaves, rinsed well balsamic cranberry sauce, or mayo

optional: whole grain or sweet & spicy mustard

the process

1. Assemble sandwich with your choice of the options.

2. If you want to prepare for the week you can freeze the sandwich with turkey, Brie, mayo and mustard.

3. Bring arugula on the side and add after your sandwich has thawed out.

crunchy hummus & veggie sandwich

This veggie sandwich leaves you satisfied and energized. The protein from the hummus combined with the complex carbohydrates of the whole grain bread is a wonderful source of energy and a great way to jumpstart your afternoon.

Ingredients (Per Serving)

2 slices	whole grain bread
2 tablespoons	homemade hummus (see page 58)
6 slices	cucumber, peeled
½	tomato, sliced
½	avocado, thinly sliced
slice	red or yellow onion
2	fresh basil leaves
pinch	salt and pepper

the process

1. Spread both sides of the bread with hummus.

2. Add a layer of cucumber, tomato, avocado, onion and basil.

3. Try toasting your bread if you are enjoying this at home.

Cut the crust off of the bread for small children and cut into quarters. Start with hummus and cucumber for the younger children and add in the other veggies as they grow.

chopped asian shrimp salad

This crunchy salad is filled with nutritious vegetables and has a light, sesame flavor. If you do not have shrimp, substitute diced chicken or tofu.

Ingredients

½ lb.	cooked shrimp, tails removed (or diced chicken or tofu), chopped roughly
2	limes, juiced
1	carrot, peeled and cut into small chunks
½ head	cabbage, sliced thin
2 handfuls	cilantro, finely chopped
1	red bell pepper, cut into ½ inch cubes
1 small	avocado, cut into cubes
½	cucumber, peeled and cut into small chunks
¼ cup	rice vinegar
1 teaspoon	sesame oil
1 tablespoon	honey
2 tablespoons	extra virgin olive oil
1 tablespoon	soy sauce
1 tablespoon	sesame seeds
pinch	salt and pepper

the process

1. Put cabbage in large bowl and add all vegetables.

2. Roughly chop shrimp on a cutting board, drizzle with a splash of rice vinegar and add salt and pepper to taste. Add to salad.

3. In a small bowl, dissolve honey in rice vinegar and stir in soy sauce, sesame oil and lime juice.

4. Toss salad with dressing and serve immediately.

Tip: If you are feeling adventurous, try ½ Japanese daikon radish instead of the cucumber.

quick quinoa tabouli

Quinoa is a superfood with all eight amino acids. It is also the highest protein grain. I like eating this at room temperature after I make it. If you are refrigerating and bringing for lunch add a bit more lemon juice, garlic and extra virgin olive oil to punch up the flavor.

Ingredients (Makes About 4 Cups)

4 cups	water, chicken, or veggie broth	1/3 cup	extra virgin olive oil
½ tablespoon	granulated garlic	pinch	salt and pepper
2 cups	quinoa		
1 cup	flat leaf parsley, minced		
1/3 cup	lemon juice		
1 cup	zucchini, shredded or minced		
1	red bell pepper, finely chopped		

the process

1. Bring water or broth to a boil with garlic.

2. Toast quinoa in a pan by placing the grains in a skillet and cooking over medium heat until brown, about three minutes.

3. Place in a small strainer and rinse.

4. Add quinoa to boiling water or broth and simmer for 15 minutes.

5. Remove from heat and fold in lemon juice, olive oil, zucchini, bell pepper and parsley. Taste for salt and pepper.

6. Serve at room temperature or chilled.

michael's hummus

My husband, Michael, has perfected hummus and we all enjoy his delicious version. His secret is to use extra lemon and not too much tahini (shhh, don't tell him I told you).

Ingredients

1 can	chickpeas, drained
¼ cup	lemon juice
1 tablespoon	tahini
2 cloves	garlic
½ teaspoon	ground cumin
⅓ - ½ cup	extra virgin olive oil
1 teaspoon	salt

hummus variations

• **roasted pepper**: Add ¼ cup roasted red bell pepper to base recipe

• **Kalamata olive**: Add ¼ cup pitted Kalamata olives

the process

1. Place all ingredients in food processor except olive oil and pulse.

2. Pour olive oil through top of processor or blender while it is on high.

3. Blend until smooth or if you want your hummus to have more texture, stop puréeing when there are tiny pieces of bean still visible.

chiara's lunch

This is my daughter Chiara's favorite lunch and a nutritious alternative to the ready-packaged lunches.

Ingredients

¼ cup	hummus
1 piece	cheese, thinly sliced
½	avocado, thinly sliced
½	tomato, thinly sliced
8-10	rice crackers

the process

1. Make little rice cracker towers by assembling a smear of hummus with a piece of cheese, avocado, and tomato.

veggie sticks with creamy dill dipping sauce

If your kids love ranch dressing, this is a much healthier veggie dip. It is also a great salad dressing. It is simple to make and the kids can help. Let them whisk all ingredients together and then pick out which vegetables they want to pack in their lunch.

Ingredients

⅓ cup	sour cream	¾ teaspoon	salt
⅓ cup	plain yogurt (non-fat or regular)	1 cup	red bell pepper, celery, carrots or
2 teaspoons	dill (dried) or 1 tablespoon fresh dill, chopped		broccoli, cut for dipping
2 teaspoons	granulated garlic		
½ teaspoon	honey		
½ tablespoon	white wine vinegar		

the process

1. Place sour cream and yogurt in a medium size bowl and whisk in remaining ingredients.

2. Stir until well blended. Keeps in refrigerator for up to a week.

3. Serve with veggie sticks.

soups

"dill"icious chicken and orzo soup

Put down that can of chicken noodle soup and give this recipe a try. It is satisfying and simple.

Ingredients (Makes 8 Bowls)

2 stalks	celery	1 ½ cups	chicken, diced (if you have leftover
3	carrots		chicken from dinner this is a great
8 cups (2 qts.)	chicken broth		place to use it)
1 ¼ cups	orzo (or other small pasta)	splash	of lemon juice or balsamic vinegar
2 big handfuls	fresh baby spinach	pinch	salt and pepper
	Parmesan, grated		
1 tablespoon	dried dill or 2 tablespoons		
	fresh dill, chopped		

the process

1. Place celery and carrots in a food processor and pulse into tiny pieces (you can also do this by hand).

2. Bring broth to a boil, add orzo and cook seven minutes.

3. After orzo has cooked, add chicken.

4. Add dill, spinach, celery and carrots. Let stand for one minute then ladle into soup bowls.

5. Finish with grated Parmesan and fresh lemon juice or balsamic vinegar and taste for salt.

lunchtime lentil soup

Don't be intimidated if you have never cooked with lentils. These tiny legumes are full of flavor, nutrient dense and cook in just 15 minutes. Check for them in the bulk section or the aisle where you find rice and beans.

Ingredients

1 tablespoon	extra virgin olive oil			
1 medium	yellow or white onion, minced	1 14.5 oz. can	crushed tomatoes
handful	cilantro, minced and extra for garnish	2	carrots, peeled and minced
4 cloves	garlic, minced	2 stalks	celery, minced
1 teaspoon	ground coriander	1	lemon (optional)
1 teaspoon	ground cumin		
3 teaspoons	curry powder		
8 cups	chicken or vegetable broth		
2 ¼ cups	dried red lentils		

the process

1. Heat olive oil in the bottom of a large pot. Add onion and sauté for two minutes.

2. Add garlic, cilantro, and spices and cook for a few more minutes.

3. Add lentils, tomatoes, and broth and bring to a boil.

4. Reduce to a simmer and cook for about 15 minutes.

5. Finish with celery and carrot for a surprising crunch, and a squeeze of lemon.

roasted butternut squash and apple soup

Butternut squash is a sweet squash that kids love and is great in soups. This soup evokes warm and cozy feelings of fall while giving a crunch of apple and a healthy dose of fiber, and vitamins A and C.

Ingredients

4 cups	(about one medium) butternut squash, peeled, cleaned and cubed, or six cups of frozen squash, cubed
5 cups	veggie or chicken broth
1 medium	yellow onion, minced
2	fall apples such as Braeburn, Gala or Fuji (one apple cut into about 8 chunks; the other apple cut into small pieces, matchstick or diced small to serve as a garnish at the end)
5 cloves	garlic, peeled
½ tablespoon	mild curry powder (use 1 tablespoon if you prefer spicier)
1 tablespoon	fresh thyme, minced (can use ½ tablespoon dried thyme)
1 cup	plain yogurt
1	lemon, zested
½	lemon, juiced
pinch	kosher salt and fresh cracked pepper
2 tablespoons	shelled pumpkin seeds for garnish

and the doctor says...

Apples and butternut squash are a tremendously healthful combination. Apples are high in both soluble and insoluble fiber, have a good amount of potassium, and even some iron. Butternut squash has lots of vitamin A, potassium, and carotenoids (important antioxidants), as well as three grams of fiber per serving. Much of the vitamin C and insoluble fiber in apples is in or just below the peel, so in general it's best if apples are eaten unpeeled, as they are in this recipe.

- *Dr. Sandy Newmark*
Center for Pediatric Integrative Medicine – Tucson, AZ

the process

Preheat oven to 350 degrees.

1. If you are peeling and cutting a whole butternut squash, stab the entire squash with a fork and place directly on oven rack for five minutes. You can then peel and cut the squash much easier.

2. Spread cubed butternut squash on a baking sheet with the garlic and sprinkle with ½ the thyme, salt, pepper and drizzle liberally with extra virgin olive oil. Roast for approximately 25 minutes or until the squash starts to turn golden.

3. Meanwhile, in a large pot heat about ½ tablespoon extra virgin olive oil and add onion.

4. Sauté over medium heat until onion starts to get soft. Add remaining thyme, curry powder, and the apple. Sauté for another few minutes then add the broth.

5. When squash is done add to the pot and simmer for another 10 minutes. Meanwhile, mix yogurt with lemon zest, lemon juice and a pinch of salt for the soup topping.

6. Turn off heat and add the soup to a blender a few cups at a time. Remember, when adding hot liquids to a blender, leave the lid slightly off and start with the speed on low (you can also use an immersion blender). Pour blended soup into a large bowl or different pot. Continue until all soup is puréed (if too thick, add more broth).

7. Serve with a dollop of the yogurt mix, a sprinkle of the apple, and shelled pumpkin seeds.

tuscan chicken soup

Making this soup in my Houston kitchen on a fall Sunday afternoon evokes memories of my time spent on a Tuscan farm. It sounds too good to be true, but these savory smells can transport you there too! Have the kids help you peel carrots and potatoes and stir. This treat can be enjoyed throughout the week in a thermos at lunch, bringing the warmth of your home to the office or school lunch table.

Ingredients

2	garlic cloves, minced
1 teaspoon	chili flakes
1 tablespoon	extra virgin olive oil
8 cups	free-range organic chicken broth
1 14.5-oz. can	Italian plum tomatoes, crushed
2 halves or 1 full	boneless skinless chicken breast cut into pieces
1 medium	Yukon Gold potato, diced
1 can	Italian white beans, chickpeas or kidney beans, drained and rinsed
2-3 stalks	red chard, cut into one-inch pieces tough ribs removed
2 large	carrots, peeled and diced
2 ribs	celery, diced
handfull	fresh Italian parsley, minced
pinch	salt
twist	pepper (for extra kick, and for garnish only)
	grated Parmesan

the process

1. In a large pot, sauté garlic and chili in extra virgin olive oil.

2. Add broth and tomatoes.

3. Add chicken.

4. After about five minutes add potato.

5. Cook on a gentle boil for about 15 minutes.

6. Add beans, chard, carrots and celery, and simmer for a few more minutes. Don't over cook.

7. Ladle into warm bowls. Finish with parsley, Parmesan, and taste for salt and pepper.

a child who eats her veggies

As the mother of an eleven-year-old daughter I have experienced the ups, downs, and frustrations of a child's developmental eating habits: the food is too big, too small, too hot, too cold, "Mom, my noodles are touching my broccoli!" It can truly be exhausting. Eating healthy and organic is a priority in our family. I have tried to instill the love of fresh, simple foods in my daughter, Chiara. From the time she was a few months old I started feeding her puréed organic produce. As she got older, I would give her the ground-up version of our dinner. Not only did this save time (no fussing with different jars and heating times) but she learned the true flavor of foods. I believe the taste of a fresh cooked squash or a vine-ripened tomato is superior to processed food. Eating this way proved to be cost effective (fresh produce can be half as much as jarred food), as well as efficient.

Most importantly, I have a child who truly loves to eat her veggies.

dinner the mom-a-licious way

You may assume that I spend hours in the kitchen making a **fabulous feast** for my family. Let me assure you, I'm usually just as exhausted as you when six o'clock rolls around. My **priority** is to get something **delicious and healthy** on the table without over-taxing myself. The **dinner recipes** I've developed here can be prepared in as few as **seven steps** but taste like you have been over the stove for hours. Pair up one of these **great dinners** with a side dish and you are on your way to a mom-a-licious meal!

salmon with tomato, corn, and basil salsa

Besides being packed with omega-3's, which are good for the heart and promote healthy brain functioning, salmon is delicious and easy to prepare. It is a wonderful fish to experiment with since it blends with so many different flavors. There is never a reason to be conventional with salmon! This recipe is great in the summer when these vegetables are at their prime. The baby grape tomatoes have the sweetest flavor. Use wild salmon. (If farm raised is all that is available, substitute chicken or another fresh fish).

Ingredients

1 lb	wild salmon
2 tablespoons	extra virgin olive oil
¼ teaspoon	red pepper flakes
2	garlic cloves, minced
1 pint	grape or cherry tomatoes, cut in half
1	cob of corn, kernels cut off
handful	fresh basil leaves, chopped
pinch	salt and pepper

the process

Preheat broiler.

1. Rub the salmon with a bit of extra virgin olive oil and kosher salt.

2. Place under broiler and cook for five to eight minutes, depending on the thickness of fish and preference.

3. Meanwhile, put remaining olive oil, garlic and red pepper flakes in a pan. Lightly sauté the garlic. DO NOT BROWN.

4. Add the tomatoes and corn and heat for one minute. Add basil and salt and pepper to taste. Put aside.

5. When salmon is done, finish with salsa.

nutritious nuggets

This is a great alternative to store-bought or fast-food chicken nuggets. It is tasty and easy to make. Brewer's (nutritional) yeast is high in vitamins B-12 and fiber and adds dimension. I've made these a few times for my daughter's class and have had rave reviews from the 5th graders.

Ingredients

1 cup	bread crumbs (I like panko, Japanese-style breadcrumbs)
1 tablespoon	granulated garlic
4 tablespoons	brewer's (nutritional) yeast
3 tablespoons	extra virgin olive oil
pinch	salt & fresh pepper
3 tablespoons	grated Parmesan cheese (optional)
4 half	chicken breasts or two whole breasts

the process

Heat oven or toaster oven to 375 degrees.

1. Mix bread crumbs, garlic, yeast, extra virgin olive oil, salt and pepper in a bowl (add Parmesan if using).

2. Place chicken between sheets of plastic wrap and pound with a kitchen mallet or heavy pan until ¼ inch thick.

3. Cut chicken into two-inch strips (if the chicken is thick, pound it out a bit more).

4. Coat chicken with the breadcrumb mixture and place on a foil-lined baking sheet. Cook for 10 minutes.

Serve with creamy dill dipping sauce (see page 125) or sweet and spicy mustard.

turkey chili

This is another way to make delicious chili without the heaviness of adding ground beef. Ground turkey breast has almost half the amount of fat as ground beef, is lower in cholesterol and has fewer calories.

Ingredients

2 tablespoons	extra virgin olive oil	1 14.5 oz. can	fire roasted organic crushed tomatoes
1 medium	yellow onion, chopped		
2 tablespoons	ground cumin	2 15 oz. cans	black beans
1-3 teaspoons	red chili flakes	2 15 oz. cans	kidney beans
3 tablespoons	fresh garlic, chopped	1 cup	water or chicken broth
1 lb.	ground turkey breast		
1 tablespoon	soy sauce		

optional: Jack or cheddar cheese, fresh onion or sour cream for topping.

the process

1. In a heavy-bottomed pot, sauté onion, cumin and pepper over medium heat with extra virgin olive oil. Do not let onions brown. As onions become soft, about five minutes, add garlic and cook about two minutes.

2. Add ground turkey. Stir and smash up turkey. Add soy sauce. Add fire-roasted tomatoes. Add beans and water or broth.

3. Bring to a boil, turn down to medium heat and cook for 10 minutes.

4. Serve with grated sharp cheddar or Jack cheese, chopped fresh onion and sour cream.

taco night

This is a fun way to get the family together. If you have taco night once a week, you can use tofu, chicken, fish, or beef on different weeks.

This version with tofu is a really clean, fresh dish. The cabbage and lime together are crispy and light.

Ingredients (Serves 6-8)

1 tablespoon	extra virgin olive oil
1 package	low-fat tofu, crumbled
½ tablespoon	garlic powder
1 teaspoon	turmeric
1 teaspoon	ground cumin
dash	hot sauce
1 teaspoon	dried oregano
1 cup	cherry tomatoes, halved or quartered
1	avocado, cubed
1 cup	green cabbage, very thinly sliced
1 package	fat-free whole wheat tortillas
1 bunch	fresh cilantro, chopped
1 bunch	green onions, thinly sliced
2	limes, quartered
2 cups	sharp cheddar cheese, shredded
1 cup	plain low-fat yogurt or sour cream (optional)

the process

1. Heat the extra virgin olive oil in a skillet. Add tofu, spices, and hot sauce and cook for a few minutes until heated through. Add salt to taste. (Cook ground chicken or lean beef with the same spices as tofu, but allow 10 more minutes).

2. Arrange tomatoes, avocado, cabbage, onions, and limes on a platter.

3. Heat tortillas.

4. Assemble the taco with your favorite ingredients.

12.

Tell someone they inspire you.

Whether it is your mom, your child, your cousin, or someone you have been too intimidated to approach — we need to support one another!

cousin molly's chicken stew, italiano style

My cousin Molly has worked in some of the top restaurants in New York City. She also spent time in kitchens in Italy. This delicious recipe is one of my favorites. It's simple, yet rich in flavor.

Ingredients (Serves 4)

1 whole	chicken, quartered (or any four parts you wish to eat)	1 ½ cups	crushed tomatoes
2 tablespoons	extra virgin olive oil	2	celery stalks, halved lengthwise and cubed
1 whole	yellow onion, thinly sliced into half moons	1 cup	chicken stock
¾ cup	carrots, peeled and diced medium	pinch	salt and pepper
1 tablespoon	minced garlic, about four cloves	splash	balsamic vinegar
		¼ cup	fresh basil, chopped

the process

1. Season chicken well with salt and pepper.

2. Heat one tablespoon of the extra virgin olive oil in a hot pan until just before smoking.

3. Add chicken, skin side down, and sear until golden brown.

4. Remove chicken, drain pan, and add one tablespoon of extra virgin olive oil. Add onions until soft, about five minutes. Add carrots and garlic until they begin to soften, about five to seven minutes. Add tomatoes and celery and let cook for a few minutes.

5. Remove the skin from the cooked chicken and add back into stew.

6. Add chicken stock and simmer for about 25 minutes.

7. Season with salt and pepper, balsamic vinegar, and fresh chopped basil.

one-dish dinner
lemony chicken with vegetables & Parmesan

This dish is so easy. It's perfect for those busy nights when making a full dinner for the family feels overwhelming. You don't have to worry about an additional side dish, and your family will get a healthy dose of vegetables.

Ingredients (Serves 4-6)

1 pound	chicken tenders (or boneless, skinless breast cut into one-inch strips)
2-3 tablespoons	garlic, minced
2-3 cups	vegetables of your choice, cut into small pieces (sweet potatoes, rutabaga, celery, carrots, broccoli, etc.)
2 tablespoons	extra virgin olive oil
1	lemon, juiced
2 tablespoons	Parmesan cheese, grated
pinch	salt and pepper

the process

Preheat oven to 400 degrees.

1. Place chicken, garlic, and vegetables in a baking dish.

2. Drizzle with lemon juice and extra virgin olive oil. Mix in the salt and pepper.

3. Top with the Parmesan cheese and bake for 15-20 minutes.

Serve and enjoy!

get the kids involved

Peeling garlic is an easy way to get the kids involved. I started Chiara when she was two-years old.

Other places you can get the little ones started on kitchen basics:

- cracking eggs

- snapping asparagus

- shelling beans

- stirring batter, sauces, and dressings

- peeling carrots (supervised around five-years old)

- zesting and grating (supervised around six-years old)

- setting the table

sesame & soy-brined chicken

Brining is similar to marinating, and is another way to keep chicken moist and flavorful. It cuts down the cooking time as well. Do not overbrine because the texture can become rubbery.

Ingredients (Serves 4)

1 ½ cups	water
3 tablespoons	tamari or soy sauce
1 teaspoon	toasted sesame oil
1 tablespoon	rice vinegar
1 tablespoon	sugar
4 half or 2 whole	boneless, skinless chicken breasts (preferably antibiotic free and organic)
drizzle	extra virgin olive oil
1 tablespoon	sesame seeds
handful	fresh cilantro

the process

1. Place the water, soy, vinegar, sugar and sesame oil in a large sealable plastic bag or a shallow glass dish. Add chicken and marinate for 15 minutes to overnight.

2. Heat oven to high broil (you can also grill).

3. Remove chicken from the brine and place on a baking sheet. Drizzle with olive oil and coat with sesame seeds.

4. Broil for approximately seven minutes if breasts are thin, or pounded. For thicker breasts, allow 12-15 minutes. Finish with cilantro and an extra splash of tamari (optional).

Serve with gingered rice & edamame (see page 115).

pinot grigio vinegar grilled chicken

Here is another favorite brine and a quick and easy way to make a versatile and flavorful chicken. This is a great chicken to have ready for lunch salads and sandwiches. Pinot Grigio wine vinegar has a distinctive crisp, apple taste.

Ingredients (Serves 4-6)

4	boneless, skinless breasts or one whole chicken cut into pieces (quartered)
½ cup	Pinot Grigio, champagne, or white wine vinegar (I use Lucini Pinot Grigio Italian Wine Vinegar)
¼ cup	salt
¼ cup	sugar
4 cups	water
¼ cup	fresh basil or mint or a combo of the two, chopped
drizzle	extra virgin olive oil
dash	salt and pepper

the process

1. Make brine by combining Pinot Grigio vinegar, sugar and salt with four cups of water in a large, resealable plastic bag. Refrigerate and soak chicken in brine mixture for two to three hours.

2. Remove chicken, add a bit of salt and pepper, brush with extra virgin olive oil and grill or broil. Time will vary from 5-10 minutes depending on thickness of chicken.

3. Finish with extra virgin olive oil and chopped fresh basil and mint.

Serve with guiltless mashed potatoes (see page 114).

lemony zucchini and basil quinoa pilaf with chicken

This one-dish dinner makes great leftovers for a fun lunch salad.

Ingredients (Serves 6)

2 tablespoons	extra virgin olive oil
1 medium	yellow onion, chopped
3	garlic cloves, minced
2 cups	quinoa, dry toasted and rinsed
4 cups	vegetable or chicken broth
2	chicken breasts, cut into 1 inch pieces
dash	salt and pepper
2	zucchini, cut into ¼ inch pieces
1 cup	basil leaves, torn
2	lemons, juiced
¼ cup	Parmesan cheese
½ cup	slivered raw almonds

the process

1. Sauté the onions and garlic in extra virgin olive oil in a medium size pot. Add quinoa, broth, chicken, and a pinch of salt and pepper.

2. Bring to a boil, cover and reduce heat to low.

3. After 15 minutes stir in zucchini, lemon juice, almonds and ¾ of the basil.

4. Turn heat off and replace lid for two minutes.

5. Finish with the remaining basil and Parmesan cheese. Add salt and pepper to taste.

homemade shake and bake

There are various boxed versions of shake and bake. This is a way to use up some of those dried spices in your cabinet without adding all the preservatives and chemicals found in many of the store-bought poultry seasonings.

Get the kids to shake the chicken in the bag.

Ingredients

½ cup	white or wheat flour, or a combination of the two
½ cup	panko (Japanese style) or regular bread crumbs
¼ cup	granulated garlic
3+ tablespoons	of combined dried spices such as paprika, celery seed, oregano, dry mustard powder, curry powder, etc.
2 tablespoons	kosher salt
¼ cup	fresh herbs such as basil, parsley or thyme or a combo, minced
4 - 6	chicken breasts or one whole chicken, cut into pieces (quartered)
drizzle	extra virgin olive oil

the process

Preheat oven to 350 degrees.

1. Place all ingredients (except chicken and extra virgin olive oil) in a large plastic bag and shake well to mix. Rinse the chicken and then shake in the bag.

2. Place the coated chicken on a foil-lined baking sheet and cook for 20 minutes to one hour, depending on the size and quantity of chicken.

3. Bake until golden brown, crispy, and juices run clear when poked with a knife. Drizzle with extra virgin olive oil afterwards.

pork tender with savory fruit

Pork has received a bad rap, but if you use pork from smaller farms like Niman Ranch or Snake River, you can rest assured that the quality will be excellent. Pork is wonderful with cooked fruits. Apricots or peaches can be substituted for the apples in the summer months.

Ingredients

1 ½ tablespoons	ground cumin	⅓ cup	water
dash	salt and pepper	2 tablespoons	fresh thyme, chopped
¾ - 1lb.	pork tenderloin		
1 tablespoon	extra virgin olive oil		
1 large	apple, cut in ½ inch slices with skin on (use a peach or two apricots when in season)		

the process

1. Coat the tenderloin with cumin, salt and pepper.

2. Heat the extra virgin olive oil in a heavy skillet.

3. When the pan is very hot, add pork, and brown both sides (approximately two minutes per side). Remove the pork and add the apples to the pan. Let the apples begin to brown while stirring.

4. Pour in water and scrape the bottom of the pan with a wooden spoon. Add thyme.

5. Push apples to the edges of the pan and put pork back in. Place lid on and simmer for seven minutes.

6. Turn off the heat and let stand for a few minutes. Slice pork and serve.

Enjoy this with cranberry, balsamic and mint relish (see page 123), and guiltless mashed potatoes (see page 114).

simple grilled beef with rosemary

This delicious, easily prepared weeknight meal can also serve as a great dinner party entree. Using an inexpensive cut such as eye-of-round or London Broil is a good way to try organic beef. You will be surprised by how flavorful this is and by using the thin slicing technique you remove the "tough" quality usually associated with lower-priced cuts of meat.

Ingredients (Serves 8)

2-3 pounds	organic beef (use a large boneless cut such as eye-of-round or London Broil)	4-5 sprigs	fresh rosemary, cleaned and finely chopped
drizzle	extra virgin olive oil	1 tablespoon	fresh Italian parsley, chopped
¼ cup	balsamic vinegar	4 cloves	garlic, minced
dash	salt and pepper		

the process

1. Heat the grill. Coat the roast with oil and vinegar, then add salt, pepper and rosemary. Place the beef on the grill and cook to desired temperature (I suggest medium rare).

2. Let the meat stand for a few minutes. Slice thin and serve with a final drizzle of the balsamic vinegar.

3. Sprinkle with parsley and more rosemary if desired. I also like to top it with sautéed garlic and hot chili flakes that have been lightly sautéed in two tablespoons extra virgin olive oil.

Tip: If you have extra beef, save it for a few days and make tacos, steak sandwiches, or salad.

pasta 101

I find in my classes that most people make several errors while cooking pasta. Thus, a little Pasta 101 is in order.

1. Generously salt your water, but don't put oil in it (it doesn't allow the pasta sauce to adhere to the pasta).

2. Don't overcook your pasta. Periodically test pasta towards the end of the suggested cooking time, it should have a slightly firm center. Don't rinse it after straining.

3. Finally, if you are going to spend time creating a sauce from scratch, use a pasta shape like a Penne Regatte, that will capture your sauce.

basic tomato sauce

This simple sauce is a staple in our house. Look for high-quality San Marzano Italian tomatoes – in my opinion they have the best flavor.

Ingredients

2 tablespoons	extra virgin olive oil
4-5 cloves	garlic, minced (not too small)
½ teaspoon	red chili flakes
1 28-oz. can	tomatoes (with no additional ingredients)
½ teaspoon	salt
1 lb.	pasta
⅓ cup	fresh basil, Italian parsley, or a combo of the two, chopped
¼ cup	fresh Parmesan cheese, grated

the process

1. Sauté garlic and chili flakes in the extra virgin olive oil. DO NOT let the garlic get brown.

2. Add tomatoes and salt and simmer for 15 minutes.

3. Bring a large pot of salted water to a boil.

4. Add pasta and cook until al dente.

5. Drain pasta (DO NOT rinse) and toss with sauce. Add parsley and basil and finish with Parmesan cheese.

butternut squash penne

A non-traditional approach to a pasta dish. Kids love the sweet taste of butternut squash. This dish is savory and full of vitamins, including a high dose of vitamins A and C.

Ingredients

1½ - 2 cups	fresh butternut squash, peeled, cleaned and cubed (or 4 bags of frozen butternut squash)	¼ cup	broth or water
		dash	salt and pepper
		1 lb.	dry pasta
		⅓ cup	Parmesan cheese, grated
3 cloves	garlic, chopped	¼ cup	toasted pumpkin seeds
2 tablespoons	extra virgin olive oil		(optional)
1 tablespoon	fresh thyme or sage (or both), chopped		

the process

1. Bring a pot of salted water to a boil. If you are peeling and cutting a whole butternut squash, pierce the entire squash with a fork. Place the squash directly on the rack in a 350-degree oven for five minutes. You can then peel and cut the squash much easier than when it is raw.

2. Cut squash into ½ inch (or smaller) cubes. Add pasta when the water is rapidly boiling.

3. Meanwhile, in a large sauté pan over medium heat, add your garlic, olive oil and ½ of the herbs and cook garlic for a few minutes. Do not brown.

4. Add squash and sauté until it starts to get soft. If it starts to stick to the pan, add a few tablespoons of water or broth to loosen.

5. Cook pasta until al dente (it should have a bit of a chew to it), drain and reserve one cup of the pasta water.

6. Add pasta to the sauté pan and moisten with the pasta water. Add the remaining herbs and ½ of the cheese.

7. Serve the remaining cheese on top of the pasta with fresh cracked pepper. Finish with toasted pumpkin seeds if using.

baked tilapia with tomato, basil, and black olives

This simple dish has a wonderful flavor. Although it is quickly prepared, it will seem like you spent hours in the kitchen.

Ingredients (Serves 4-5)

1½ pints	grape tomatoes, halved	1 teaspoon	dried chili flakes
2-3 cloves	minced garlic	pinch	salt to taste
½ cup	black olives pitted and chopped	drizzle	extra virgin olive oil
	(Kalamata and nicoise are also good)	1½ lbs.	tilapia
1 handful	fresh basil, chopped		

the process

Pre-heat oven to 475 degrees.

1. In a small bowl, mix the tomatoes with garlic, olives, basil, chili, salt and a drizzle of extra virgin olive oil.

2. Make an "envelope" out of foil or parchment and place ½ of the tomato mixture on the bottom.

3. Lay the fish on the mixture and top with more of the tomato mixture.

4. Seal "envelope" and place on a baking sheet.

5. Bake for approximately 20 minutes.

6. Remove from oven and allow to stand for a few minutes before serving.

Serve with guiltless mashed potatoes (see page 114), or smashed roasted cauliflower (see page 119).

roasted cumin-rubbed snapper

w / pineapple and cilantro salsa

This is a great dish in the summer months. The tropical salsa cools you down and keeps the heat out of the kitchen.

Ingredients

roasted cumin-rubbed snapper

1 tablespoon	toasted whole cumin seed, ground or smashed with a mortar and pestle (can substitute pre-ground cumin)
½ tablespoon	brown sugar
1 teaspoon	ground turmeric
dash	ground or smashed coriander
dash	salt and pepper
2 tablespoons	extra virgin olive oil
1 ¼ lb.	fresh snapper

pineapple and cilantro salsa

1 ½ cups	pineapple (can sub one mango or mix the two)
1	fresh pepper such as jalapeño or serrano, minced* (remove the seeds to cut back on the heat)
1 small	shallot, minced
½ cup	cilantro, roughly chopped
1	lime, juiced
½ tablespoon	toasted ground cumin (or pre-ground cumin)
½	avocado, cut into small cubes
drizzle	extra virgin olive oil
pinch	salt

the process

Pre heat oven to 450 degrees.

1. Mix dry spices and olive oil together and rub onto fish.

2. Place fish on foil-lined baking sheet

3. Roast for approximately eight minutes (depending on oven and thickness of fish).

the process

1. Toss pineapple with pepper, shallot, cilantro, lime juice, cumin and avocado.

2. Drizzle with extra virgin olive oil to moisten and add salt to taste.

3. Serve over the fish or on the side.

* Be careful when mincing a hot pepper. The spicy juices absorb easily into your skin and can sting. Rub a bit of olive oil on your hands before handling to create a barrier.

a salad that eats like a meal

Another great recipe from my talented cousin, Molly. This salad is filling, but fruity. Kale is a great source of folic acid and vitamins A and C.

Ingredients

1 15-oz. can	(about 1 ½ cups) black beans	½ cup	Jack cheese, finely cubed
1 tablespoon	ground cumin	1	avocado, cubed
pinch	salt and pepper	½ bunch	radishes, sliced
½ bunch	kale, cleaned, dried and finely chopped	1 bunch	scallions, sliced into thin rounds
		1 small	jicama, diced
2 cups	romaine lettuce, cleaned, dried, and chopped	½ cup	cilantro, chopped
		½	mango, diced
1 cup	tomatoes, diced (or a handful of cherry tomatoes, halved)	2	limes, juiced
		2 tablespoons	extra virgin olive oil

the process

1. Warm and season black beans with salt and a tablespoon of cumin in a sauté pan over medium heat. Put aside.

2. Toss all other ingredients together in a large bowl.

3. Top with beans and creamy dill dressing (see page 125).

ginger-tofu stir-fry

I married a man who was raised in Texas on beef. His perception of tofu as one of those wacky California hippie foods seems rather common. With this recipe, I have made converts of many people, including my husband. Tofu is high in protein but mild in flavor so it easily combines with a variety of flavors. If you like a "meatier" texture, freeze the tofu and then thaw it.

Ingredients (Serves 4-6)

2 tablespoons	extra virgin olive oil	1	carrot, cut into thin strips
2 cups	mushrooms, sliced	1 rib	celery, peeled and cut into ½
2 tablespoons	fresh ginger, grated		inch pieces
½ medium	yellow onion, peeled and cut	2 generous handfuls	snow peas
	into thin half circles	1 tablespoon	low sodium soy sauce
2 ½ cups	fresh or frozen broccoli,	6 oz.	low-fat tofu, cubed
	chopped	dash	salt

the process

1. In a wok, heat extra virgin olive oil and add onion and ginger. Sauté for about three minutes over medium heat.

2. Add mushrooms and cook until moisture evaporates (about three minutes).

3. Add broccoli, carrots, celery and snow peas, and stir for a few minutes. Add the soy sauce, stirring frequently.

4. Add the tofu and cook until warmed through. Add salt to taste.

Serve with gingered rice & edamame (see page 115).

My oldest friend, Franny, has been making her dogs' food for years. Now with our dogs, Zoe and Henna, I see the great value in taking the time to supplement our pets' meals with some nutritious, home-cooked food. When our dog, Zoe, was a puppy she was very ill and not responding to any over-the-counter food. I tried some basic home-cooked foods and within a week she was putting on weight and her coat was glistening. Now, I make a big batch and freeze it in smaller containers, saving time and money.

Always check with your veterinarian to make sure that the food you are going to make is appropriate for your dog's breed, weight and age.

mom-a-licious pet

zoe and henna's doggy dinner

Ingredients

2 parts	free-range chicken
1 part	ground organic beef, lamb, or turkey
1 part	organic veggie mix (some or all of the following): sweet potato, zucchini (raw & grated), peas, carrots
½ tablespoon	(each) mix-ins to individual portions of the cooked food before serving (for a 35-40 pound dog): organic plain yogurt, brewer's yeast, extra virgin olive oil, flax oil

the process

1. Put all ingredients in a pot (if you are using zucchini, keep it aside and put in last). Cover with water by two inches.

2. Bring to a boil and then turn down to a simmer. Cook until chicken is no longer pink.

3. Let cool a bit then add to food processor in batches (make sure there are no bones). Store in airtight containers in the refrigerator for up to three days or make a large amount and freeze in individual containers. Defrost overnight in the refrigerator. Do not microwave.

4. Add a bit of warm water or broth before serving and add a portion of the "mix-ins."

Top things NOT to feed your dog

Grapes or raisins…they cause liver damage, onions and garlic cause anemia, as well as liver damage. Also avoid: chocolate, cooked bones, sugar, salt, raw salmon, and raw eggs.

Things to do

- Add fresh food to your kibble mix (cooked chicken, beef, lamb, turkey) preferably organic. Avoid giving your dogs the growth hormones and antibiotics in factory-farmed meats; check different websites for more info.

- Use the following veggies in their raw form: (remember to keep the veggies in a smaller ratio to the protein) Chopped parsley; alfalfa sprouts; finely grated carrots with peel; finely grated zucchini and other soft squash with peel; lettuce and mixed greens; finely grated beets (don't be alarmed if their urine or stool turns pink!)

- Cook the following veggies: corn; peas; green beans; broccoli; cauliflower; hard winter squash; potatoes

Eat and serve local and organic
as much as possible

Grow something fresh
and use it – whether you have a
large garden or one potted herb.

a side of mom-a-licious

A **six-year old** nephew who **eats Brussels sprouts**. A four-year old on his third helping of corn. A previously leafy green phobic **mother** who now **makes chard at least once a week** for her family. These are true stories that have risen from the following recipes. You will be **amazed** by how your family's **relationship with vegetables** will start to **transform** when making these a normal part of your meals. If your two-year old turns her nose up on her first taste of roasted root vegetables, **don't give up** – a second try can end up being the beginning of a **new favorite**.

sesame and soy-roasted fall vegetables

This dish is visually stunning, absolutely delicious, and packed with nutrition. Don't be intimidated by the variety of root vegetables, they are easy to prepare. In fact, you should be aware of the incredible health benefits these vegetables offer, including vitamin A (carrots) and beta carotene (sweet potatos). Health benefits include lowering cholesterol (parsnips), and anti-carcinogen effects (turnips).

Ingredients

1 tablespoon	sesame seeds	1	sweet potato or garnet yam, peeled and cut into one-inch wedges
1 tablespoon	toasted sesame oil	1 cup	carrots, peeled and cut into one-inch pieces
1 tablespoon	granulated garlic		
¼ cup	tamari, soy or Bragg's liquid aminos	1 medium	red onion, cut into ⅛'s
⅓ cup	extra virgin olive oil	1	parsnip or turnip, one-inch cubes
1 cup	butternut squash, peeled and cut into one-inch cubes	twist	fresh cracked pepper

the process

Pre-heat oven to 400 degrees.

1. Mix the sesame seeds and oil, extra virgin olive oil, tamari and garlic together.

2. Put all the vegetables in a large bowl and coat with the sesame and soy mix.

3. Spread on an oiled baking sheet, sprinkle with fresh cracked pepper and roast for 20 minutes. Stir vegetables around on the tray with a spatula or wooden spoon and roast for 10-15 more minutes or until golden.

If you have extra marinade you can store in the refrigerator for up to two weeks and use on chicken or fish. Great with the sesame and soy-brined chicken.

balsamic-roasted chard

Chard is one of those intimidating vegetables for many of the moms I teach. Once you make this recipe, all fear will be gone! It is one of the most vitamin rich veggies, packed with vitamin C and iron. I have had many skeptics transformed by this simple and delicious preparation.

Ingredients

1-2 heads	Swiss chard, chopped in 1-2 inch strips with tough ribs removed
drizzle	extra virgin olive oil
pinch	kosher salt
big splash	balsamic vinegar

the process

Pre-heat oven to 400 degrees.

1. Lay chopped chard out on a sheet pan. Drizzle with extra virgin olive oil until chard is lightly coated.

2. Sprinkle with Kosher salt. Roast for approximately five minutes.

3. Remove and drizzle with balsamic vinegar to taste.

guiltless mashed potatoes

Normally, mashed potatoes evoke thoughts of coziness, warmth, and comfort, but also indulgence and guilt! In this recipe, you get all the benefits of comfort food, but no guilt. Surprisingly, this delicious version involves no milk or butter and yet retains its creamy, satisfying nature via the Yukon Gold potatoes.

Ingredients

6 large	Yukon Gold potatoes, peeled and cut into large chunks
1 box	(or four cups) chicken broth
1-2 cups	water
3-5 cloves	garlic
pinch	salt and pepper
½ cup	Parmesan cheese

the process

1. Place potatoes in pot with broth, a bit of salt, and garlic cloves. Add water to cover two inches above the potatoes.

2. Bring potatoes to a boil and cook until soft, but not falling apart.

3. Drain most of the liquid into a large measuring cup. Smash potatoes with a hand masher, whisk or with electric beaters.

4. Add Parmesan cheese and extra broth/water until you reach desired consistency. Finish with fresh cracked black pepper.

easy roasted asparagus

This is by far one of the easiest and tastiest vegetables to put on the table with dinner. Packed with vitamin A, you can rest assured that your family is getting a good dose of nutrients.

Ingredients

1 bunch	asparagus, snapped at ends
drizzle	extra virgin olive oil
pinch	kosher salt

the process

Preheat oven to 400 degrees.

1. Lay asparagus out on a cookie sheet.

2. Drizzle generously with extra virgin olive oil and sprinkle with kosher salt.

3. Depending on thickness of asparagus, cook for 5-10 minutes.

gingered rice & edamame

Edamame beans are high in protein and a favorite with kids. Most families are familiar with these beans by now. However, if you are not, add them to your diet in this dish or as a high-protein snack with a shake of salt – delicious! Ginger adds a snappy flavor and aids in digestion. The combination together is fresh and fun.

Ingredients

2 cups	short-grain brown rice or sushi rice
2 tablespoons	fresh ginger, peeled and minced
3½ - 3¾ cups	water
1 cup	frozen edamame beans, shelled
pinch	salt
splash	tamari
¼ - ½ cup	cilantro, chopped

the process

1. If you have a rice cooker, place all ingredients in except edamame. If not, bring water, rice and ginger to a boil.

2. Turn down to low, cover with a tight lid, and cook 25 minutes for sushi rice or 35 minutes for brown rice.

3. Toss edamame in when rice is almost cooked.

4. Cover and let stand. Serve with cilantro and tamari.

pot o' beans

Italian white beans or Cannellini beans are very high in manganese, fiber, and protein and combine with a variety of flavors easily.

Ingredients

½ tablespoon	extra virgin olive oil
½ small	onion, chopped
1 pinch	chili flakes
1 tablespoon	savory herb (thyme, sage or combination of both), finely chopped
1 tablespoons	garlic, finely chopped
3 cans	Italian white beans, drained and rinsed
½ cup	chicken broth
¼ cup	purèed tomatoes
handful	chopped parsley for garnish
dash	salt

the process

1. Drizzle bottom of heavy-bottomed pot with extra virgin olive oil.

2. Stir in onions, herbs and chili flakes. Cook onions until soft, about five minutes and then add garlic.

3. Sauté for two more minutes. Add beans, tomatoes and chicken broth.

4. Cook for five minutes and serve with chopped parsley, cracked black pepper, and salt to taste.

cumin-roasted corn

This is a family favorite at my house...you may want to double or triple this recipe if you have corn lovers in your family.

Ingredients

16-oz. package	frozen organic corn (or four fresh ears of corn, kernels removed)
3 tablespoons	extra virgin olive oil
1 tablespoon	ground cumin
pinch	salt and pepper

the process

Heat oven to 400 degrees.

1. Spread corn on a large rimmed baking sheet. Sprinkle with cumin, olive oil, salt and pepper.

2. Roast for 15 minutes (or longer if you want a bit crispy).

smashed roasted cauliflower and herbs

A great winter side dish with many possibilities. Serve it as your weeknight dinner vegetable (kids love it!), bring it with great bread to a party as a wonderful appetizer spread, or toss it with pasta and add a little cream and Parmesan and you have a savory, warm supper. This is so delicious, you may want to double the recipe.

Ingredients

1 head	cauliflower
5 cloves	garlic, peeled and cut in ½ lengthwise (use more if you want the extra flavor)
⅓ cup	extra virgin olive oil
¼ cup	fresh herbs (dill, Italian parsley, thyme, and basil are all great), chopped
pinch	salt and pepper

the process

Preheat oven to 400 degrees.

1. Remove the greenery from the cauliflower and the core. Cut in ½ lengthwise then rough cut into small ½ inch chops. Lay cauliflower and garlic on a large rimmed baking sheet.

2. Drizzle with the extra virgin olive oil.

3. Generously salt and pepper.

4. Bake for approximately 25 minutes (or until very soft and starting to brown).

5. Put cauliflower and herbs in a food processor and pulse until chunky, but do not over-process. You can smash it with a potato masher as well.

not your mama's brussels sprouts

Not to say your mama wasn't doing a good job with the Brussels sprouts, it is just that this recipe actually makes you want to eat them.

Ingredients

1 bag (about 2 cups)	Brussels sprouts
2 tablespoons	extra virgin olive oil
1	shallot, finely minced (or ¼ medium onion)
½ teaspoon	dried red chili flakes
2 cloves	garlic, minced (optional)

1 tablespoon	fresh thyme (or rosemary, or a combination), minced
2 tablespoons	water
pinch	salt and pepper

the process

1. Cut the tough bottom off the sprout, then cut in half lengthwise (remove outer leaves if they are damaged).

2. Pour enough extra virgin olive oil in the bottom of a skillet to coat it. Turn on medium high heat.

3. Add shallot and chili flakes, sauté until soft, about two minutes (if using garlic add at this point).

4. Add sprouts and half the thyme and cook until they start to brown, turning occasionally (will take about 10 minutes to cook).

5. If the sprouts seem to be sticking to the pan and getting a bit dry, add a couple tablespoons of water to loosen them up.

6. Sprinkle with remaining thyme, salt to taste, and serve.

sun-dried tomato pesto

Sun-dried tomatoes are sweet and add a rich flavor to any sauce or dip.

Ingredients

1 cup	sun-dried tomatoes packed in oil, drained
¼ cup	Parmesan cheese, freshly grated
½ cup - ¾ cup	extra virgin olive oil
¼ cup (packed)	fresh basil leaves
¼ cup (packed)	fresh parsley leaves
¼ cup	pine nuts
2	garlic cloves, crushed under a knife and peeled
dash	fresh ground pepper

cranberry, balsamic & mint relish

This is a refreshing twist on a traditional cranberry relish. It is also great as a spread for turkey sandwiches, add some arugula and brie cheese on delicious crusty bread and you have a savory sandwich in minutes. This is also a great addition to roasted pork loin.

Ingredients

1 12 oz bag	cranberries
¾ cup	brown sugar
¾ cup	Balsamic vinegar
¼ cup	fresh mint leaves
1	orange, zested
½ inch piece	fresh ginger, peeled

mixed-herb pesto

This pesto will stay fresh for up to a week in the refrigerator and can be used as a dip, on sandwiches, or on pasta.

Ingredients

2 tablespoons	pine nuts, toasted
2 large	cloves garlic
1 ½ cups	fresh flat leaf parsley
1 cup	mixed fresh herbs (mint, basil, dill, oregano, or thyme)
½ cup	freshly grated Parmesan cheese
⅓ cup	extra virgin olive oil
pinch	salt

the process

1. Process all the ingredients and half of the extra virgin olive oil in a food processor fitted with the metal blade.

2. Slowly pour in the remaining oil as the pesto is processing.

3. Blend until the mixture forms a coarse paste; add more oil if you desire a thinner paste.

the process

1. Place all ingredients in the food processor.

2. Pulse until well blended and pieces are about as big as rice.

3. Refrigerate and enjoy for up to one week.

the process

1. Put all ingredients except oil in food processor. Begin to pulse.

2. With processor on, slowly pour oil through food chute. Process until well blended.

3. Spoon into an airtight container. Store in refrigerator for up to one week or freeze.

pineapple and cilantro salsa

Salsas are a great place to experiment with ingredients – depending on what season or region of the country you are in, you can use mango, pineapple, different chilies, etc. This recipe is great with fish, chicken, or tacos.

Ingredients

1½ cups	pineapple (can substitute one mango or mix the two)
1	fresh pepper such as jalapeno or serrano, minced* (remove the seeds to cut back on the heat)
1 small	shallot, minced
½ cup	cilantro, roughly chopped
1	lime, juiced
drizzle	extra virgin olive oil
½ tablespoon	toasted ground cumin
½	avocado, cut into small cubes
dash	salt

the process

1. Toss pineapple with pepper, shallot, cilantro, lime juice, cumin and avocado. Drizzle with extra virgin olive oil to moisten, add salt to taste.

* Be careful when mincing a hot pepper. The spicy juices from hot peppers absorb easily into your skin and can sting. Rub a bit of olive oil on your hands before handling to create a barrier.

creamy dill dressing and dipping sauce

This can be used for multiple foods, including children's snacks, salad dressing, sandwiches, and vegetable dip.

Ingredients

⅓ cup	sour cream
⅓ cup	plain kefir (can substitute plain yogurt)
2 teaspoons	dried dill or 1 tablespoon fresh dill, chopped
1 ½ teaspoons	granulated garlic
½ teaspoon	honey
½ tablespoon	white wine vinegar
¾ teaspoon	salt

the process

1. Place sour cream and yogurt in a medium size bowl, whisk in all other ingredients, stir until well blended.

Dressing will keep in refrigerator for a week.

Go out with your friends regularly,
let off steam, make memories, and
come home grateful for your family.

feeding baby the mom-a-licious way

Finicky eating and **children** supposedly go hand-in-hand. What if I were to tell you both from experience and current studies that if introduced into the diet early enough your child will **enjoy the exotic taste of** cardamom and cumin? How about dark **leafy greens** like kale, basil, and seaweed? If I now tell you that it is **easy to make** your own baby food, you have to admit that it is worth a try. More importantly, by introducing **unique and fresh flavors** to your baby now you may be saving yourself the hassle of picky eating down the road.

taste beginnings

Renowned pediatrician Dr. Alan Greene of Stanford University says that taste beginnings is one of the keys to building a foundation of healthy eating for your child. He teaches us that just as early childhood is a unique window of time for learning the subtle sounds of a spoken language, it is also a unique window for learning the spices and flavors of our culture. "One of the reasons that babies are apt to put almost anything in their mouths is that they are so eager to sample and learn their palates. Their brains are primed to taste and remember. What a waste to squander this opportunity on over-refined white flour rice cereal and over-processed jars of glop!"

Compared to the bland, over-processed and discolored veggies that are in baby foods today, the fresh baby food that you will learn to prepare in this section will be the envy of moms all around you, and most importantly, your child will benefit. There is no comparison to fresh cooked spinach, peas, or squash when it comes to taste or nutrition.

People have always been amazed at my daughter's desire for vegetables. She enjoys the kind of vegetables that most kids wouldn't even try, including: kale, Brussels sprouts, cabbage, and butternut squash. I attribute her liberal palate to her earliest experience with food and being "trained" to taste true flavors.

banana-rama

Children love bananas, and here is a way to add millet, a nutritious grain that is heart-healthy with an abundance of magnesium.

Ingredients

1 cup	water
pinch	cinnamon
¼ cup	millet
2	ripe bananas, mashed

the process

1. In a small pot bring water and cinnamon to a boil.
2. Add millet. Cook until soft, about 15 minutes.
3. Fold in bananas. Divide into small containers.
4. Cool and serve.

Freeze extra or keep in refrigerator for up to three days. Add a bit of warm water to change temperature.

pear and basil smash

Adding an herb such as basil brings a boost of flavor and starts exercising those taste buds. Basil also adds extra vitamin K.

Ingredients

4	ripe organic pears (Bartlett, D-Anjou, or Bosc), peeled and cut (around the core) into one-inch chunks
2 teaspoons	fresh basil, chopped (about 2 large leaves)
¼ cup	water

the process

1. Place the pears in a pot with the water.
2. Steam pears for about 10 minutes, until soft when poked with a fork.
3. Purèe in a food processor with the basil.
4. Cool and serve.

"glorious" greens

These greens are so high in nutrients, including iron and vitamins A, C, and K, you'll make your pediatrician proud!

Ingredients

½ lb.	baby organic spinach, rinsed
1 bunch	kale, rinsed, tough ribs removed and rough chopped
pinch	seaweed, arame, or hijiki
¼ cup	whole milk organic plain yogurt
pinch	turmeric

the process

1. Place wet kale in a large pot with a small amount of water (about a ¼ inch).

2. Steam for about five minutes with lid on.

3. Add spinach and replace lid. Cook for another three to five minutes.

4. Remove and place greens, yogurt, and tumeric in a food processor and purèe.

5. Cool and serve.

butternut squash and lentils

Butternut squash is a sweet squash that babies tend to love. Adding lentils provides a high amount of fiber, folate, iron and protein.

Ingredients

2 cups	fresh butternut squash, cut into chunks or 3 cups frozen butternut squash
½ cup	red lentils, rinsed
4 cups	water
⅓ teaspoon	cardamom

the process

1. Place all ingredients in a sauce pan and bring to a boil.

2. Turn down to simmer and cook until soft, about 20 minutes.

3. Purèe in a food processor.

4. Cool and serve.

avocado-quinoa mash

Avocados are one of my favorite foods for babies. High in vitamins A and E, they are also packed with heart-protecting monounsaturated fats. Mash them with banana, peas, or quinoa and you have a great start for the little one.

Ingredients

1 ripe	avocado, pit removed
½ cup	quinoa, rinsed
1 cup	spring water
½ tsp.	granulated garlic

the process

1. Place water and quinoa in a pot and bring to a boil. Turn down to a simmer and cook until soft, about 15 minutes.

2. While quinoa is cooking place avocado in a bowl and smash with a fork or whisk with the garlic.

3. When quinoa is cooled add to the avocado and mix together. Store in refrigerator for two days or in freezer for two months.

15.

Make time to build health and strength.

We want to be around to enjoy our kids

and set the example that health is essential.

Plus, it is fun and energizing to get your body moving!

resources

family health

Dr. Alan Greene, MD, FDAA

author, *Raising Baby Greene*

www.drgreene.com

Dr. Mehmet Oz

co-author, *You: On A Diet*

www.oprah.com

Dr. Sandy Newmark

Center for Pediatric Integrative Medicine (Tucson, AZ)

www.drnewmark.com

Sally Fallon

author, *Nourishing Traditions*

food

Lucini Italia

www.lucini.com

extra virgin olive oil, aged 10-year balsamic, Pinot Grigio vinegar, sauces, soups

Blis

www.Blis.com

organic maple syrup, sea salt, line-caught tuna

The World's Healthiest Foods

www.theworldshealthiestfoods.com

style

Alicia Catelli

www.AliciaCatelli.com

jewelry

creative

IMAGE202 ENTERTAINMENT

www.IMAGE202.com

web, motion, audio, photography, identity

For more information on resources visit
www.mom-a-licious.com

bio

domenica catelli has positively influenced the way millions of families eat and prepare food across the United States with her tasty, easy, and healthy approach to cooking. Her claim to fame is getting children to eat rare vegetables like Brussels sprouts, Swiss chard and cauliflower, without hiding the ingredients!

Domenica is the national spokesperson for the Organic Trade Association's national campaign, "Go Organic! for Earth Day." She is a featured chef on Fox News in Houston for the "Fox Grill," where she educates viewers with her ingenuity and humor. She is an Iron Chef Judge, a guest on iVillage and "Oprah and Friends," with Dr. Oz on XM radio, and has been featured in Vegetarian Times, Kiwi Magazine, and Oprah.com. She is among a select few accomplished chefs entrusted to cook for celebrities such as Oprah Winfrey, Montel Williams, Thandie Newton, and George and Barbara Bush.

Domenica is a member of the chef advisory board of the non-profit organization Common Threads along with other celebrity chefs including Jamie Oliver, Paula Deen, and Tyler Florence. Over her career, many exclusive chefs have turned to her expertise when developing recipes. Domenica's contributions can be seen in the James Beard award-winning cookbook, Back to the Table, by Art Smith and on products in tens of thousands of grocery stores nationwide.

During her childhood in Sonoma county wine country, her senses were filled with the memories of fresh, seasonal food. She oversaw several restaurants in California from Laguna Beach to the beautiful Mendocino coast, where she was executive chef of the organic restaurant Raven's at the Stanford Inn with featured recipes from the estate's three-acre garden. Now, as a devoted mother she shares her inspiration and skills with families throughout the country. Whether she is teaching children and communities through organizations such as Recipe for Success, or creating easy guides for healthy nutrition and living, Domenica Catelli continues to bring the joys of being mom-a-licious into her own family and into the lives of others.

index

Michael: My husband, friend, and voice of reason. Your strength, integrity, and support have given me the courage and springboard from which to follow my dreams. I love you and am so grateful for our life together.

Chiara: My daughter. You said, "There would be no mom-a-licious without me," and you are right! I am so blessed to have you for my daughter. Thank you for inspiring me daily, for your kind heart, quick wit, and for eating your veggies.

Celia: There would be no "mom-a-licious" without Chiara, but there would be no book without you! You are the best editor, cheerleader, inspiration and soul sister I could ask for. Thank you for always believing in me and helping me reignite my own mom-a-licious spark. Let this be the first in a life time of projects together.

Mom: Thank you for setting an example of hard work, creativity in the kitchen, love of gardening, flowers, and friends. I love you.

Dad: Thank you for exposing me to the kitchen from my first 24 hours on this earth. Thank you for tirelessly driving to the store, airport, and after-school carpool. Whenever I've needed you on a moments notice, you've been there, I love you.

Margaret: Thank you for all the time and resources you provide for our family. Thank you for caring for Henna and Zoe. I have been blessed to have you for a mother-in-law. If only you would eat organic - I'd have it all.

Phil: Thank you for your love and support and kindness.

Constance: Thank you for being a compass in all things style. Your dedication and help with this project and my career over the years has been invaluable. Your friendship is a gift. Who knew what would be born out of that garage in south Florida!

Elliot: The "eagle eye." Your help as a friend, trainer, and mentor are such a blessing. I am so grateful to you, especially for all the prayers. LY!

Jen: You are an "angel." Thank you for sharing Evan and Chloe. Thank you for always being there for me. Your friendship has been one of my greatest anchors in Houston.

The team at FOX Houston: Kathy Williams for giving me a chance. Dart, for the support. Christy, for keeping me on. Jan, Jose, Patty, Tom and Reuben for helping me on air. Greg and Caroline for the behind-the-scenes work.

Betty: Thanks for supporting me through hair and relationships for the past six years! I am so grateful to you.

Bill: You are my voice of encouragement in this crazy process. Thank you for including me in MOL. I am inspired daily by your attitude and tenacity.

Women whom I am grateful to for love and support over the years: Amy P, Amy L, Amanda G, Jane, Rebecca, Shelly, Karen, Aileen, Holly K, Holly M, Carolyn, Monica P, Talitha, Gina, Deborah, Libby, Jill, Urania, Susan Rey, Chiara, Heather, Jenny, Sue Anne, Julie, Tanya, Kendall, Kinder, Jennifer, Michelle, Kim Y., Janie, Georgia, Porche, Patty, Liz J., and Kristen.

Sheesha: Thank you for being such a loving and supportive sister. Your talent as a jewelry artist is incredible. Your palette is phenomenal and your presence in my life, a gift.

Nicholas: You are like sunshine. I am so blessed to have you for my brother. I am so proud of you. Your easy going and loving nature are inspirational.

Matt: Thank you for sharing Celia with me during this project. For your love and support over the years and for being such a super h-uncle.

Cousins Anthony and David: Your humor makes me laugh even when we aren't together. Thank you for supporting me in my cooking endeavors over the years. I would marry either one of you if we weren't cousins.

Kim: For your support through the years. Thank you for the tag line for the cover, introducing me to Art, and being a catalyst for my career.

Dana: Your creative talent, work ethic, generous heart, and love have been a blessing. Thank you for bringing me back to cooking a decade ago and for keeping me afloat during editing week.

Mr. & Mrs. P: for providing a home-away-from home for the past 25 years. I appreciate, love and admire you both so much.

Jeannie: I can't sit at my sewing machine without thinking of you! Thank you for helping shape my understanding of the domestic life. I am so grateful for your love and optimistic perspective that always brightens my day, and thank you for my brother and sister.

Cousin Molly: Thank you for your delicious recipes and for inspiring me with your great culinary creations. Maybe you will meet Tori now.

Franny: I think that an entire lifetime of friendship and the same birthday qualifies us as family. Your support, discernment, generosity, and fantastic style are a touchstone in my life.

GP: Hon, there is no food I would rather be eating than yours! Thank you for 25 amazing years of friendship. I am so excited for 25 more of laughs, food, travels and faith.

Lei: Thank you for two decades of friendship. The support you and Adam provided for Chiara in her early years was so crucial. Your creativity, intelligence, and phenomenal ability to encourage and manage others inspires me to be a better person. Hon, you are so mom-a-licious!

Lizzy: Thank you for turning over your house for the photo shoot and mostly thanks for being my friend for 20 years.

Josh: Thank you for always being an inspiration for style. Thank you for your support of this project over the past decade. Thank you for sharing your beautiful daughter and thank you for your friendship, I love you.

Rachel: It doesn't get much more mom-a-licious than you! Your inner and outer beauty are amazing. Your strength and spark are an inspiration. I am grateful and blessed for our friendship.

Art: Thank you for your support and friendship over the years. I am so grateful to you for introducing me to so many fantastic people. Your fabulous and beautiful culinary creations are like no others. I am so proud of all the growth you have had over the past six years; you inspire me to reach further.

Renee and Daniel: The only thing better than LPS is your friendship. I love you guys.

Govind: It doesn't get much tastier than Table 8. I love your food and our friendship.

Joan and Jeff: Thank you for taking a chance on me all those years ago. Stanford Inn and Raven's will always be a treasured memory and experience.

Candy: Your advice and coaching has made me so much more mom-a-licious, thank you!

Tyler: Your energy and ideas are phenomenal. Thank you for all your support.

Marty: I am so lucky to have you to call family, whether you are challenging me or cheering me on, you help me grow and I love you for that.

Bootsy: What a blessing to have you for my sister-in-law! You're positive attitude and loving nature are a bright spot in my life.

All the kids who showed up and ate their veggies: Ruthanna, Mary Abigail, Dara, Dami, Evan, Chloe, Hudson, Joy, Lillie, Emma, Devi, Madigan, Gabriel, Gabrielle, Lola, Sammy, Skylar, Kali, Eden, Max, Justin, Beau, Claire, Colin, Catherine, Alex, Miguel, Sofia, Jackson, Kaden, and Moriah.

Nancy: Thank you for being so stylish and supportive. I love you.

Bill and Sandi: Thank you for your encouragement, inspiration and friendship. I appreciate you both so much!

Dr. Greene and Cheryl: Thank you for supporting this project and being role models.

Oprah: Thank you for the honor of sharing my cooking with you, your friends, and family over the years. Times spent at Promised Land are among my most treasured memories. You have motivated me to live up to my potential. Your life inspires my walk of faith, hard work, and perseverance.

St. Andrews Presbyterian church in Marin City (Pastor Goines) and Second Baptist, Houston (Pastor Ben Young). Your prayers and encouragement have been an anchor over the years.

IMAGE202 Entertainment: DK, Adam and Talitha. Thank you for letting me push this project to the limit. I am extremely grateful for your creativity, enthusiasm, and patience. Thank you for helping me to turn this dream into a reality.

16.

Live with gratitude.
Whether it is taking time when you
wake up, before you eat or at the end of the day,
take note of your blessings and give thanks!